CROCK·POT
◆ THE ORIGINAL SLOW COOKER ◆

Slow Cooker
Recipes

Publications International, Ltd.

Pictured on the front cover: Asian Beef Stew *(page 184)*.
Pictured on the back cover (from top): Shrimp Louisiana-Style *(page 162)*, Triple Chocolate Fantasy *(page 50)*, Ham and Cheese Pasta Bake *(page 88)* and Spicy Orange Chicken Nuggets *(page 180)*.

Preparation/cooking times: Preparation times are based on the approximate amount of time required to assemble the recipe before cooking, baking, chilling, or serving. These times include preparation steps such as measuring, chopping, and mixing. The fact that some preparation and cooking can be done simultaneously is taken into account. Preparation of optional ingredients and serving suggestions is not included.

Your **CROCK-POT®** slow cooker can be the best kitchen assistant you've ever had. Your family will enjoy delicious meals, while you save time and effort, thanks to the flavorful cooking process that works while you're away from home. To get the most from your **CROCK-POT®** slow cooker, just keep the following hints and tips in mind.

Stirring

Due to the nature of slow cooking, there's no need to stir the food unless the recipe method says to do so. In fact, taking the lid off to stir food causes your **CROCK-POT®** slow cooker to lose a significant amount of heat, which extends the cooking time. Therefore, it's best not to remove the lid.

Adding Ingredients at the End of Cooking Time

Certain ingredients are best added toward the end of the cooking time. These include:

● *Milk, sour cream, and yogurt:* Add during last 15 minutes.

● *Seafood and fish:* Add during last 30 to 60 minutes.

● *Fresh herbs:* Fresh herbs, such as basil, will turn black with extended cooking time, so if you want colorful fresh herbs, add those during the final 15 minutes of cooking.

Pasta and Rice

For best results with rice, always use converted rice. Most recipes suggest adding pasta or rice halfway through the cooking time, for best texture. If the rice doesn't seem completely cooked after the suggested time, you may add an extra ½ cup to 1 cup of liquid per cup of rice and extend the cooking time by 30 to 60 minutes.

CONTENTS

Herbs and Spices

When cooking with your **CROCK-POT®** slow cooker, use whole herbs and spices, rather than crushed or ground. The flavor and aroma of crushed or ground herbs may lessen during the extended cooking time. Be sure to taste the finished dish and add more seasonings if needed. If you prefer using colorful fresh herbs, add them during the last 15 minutes of cooking.

Cooking for Larger Quantity Yields

If you want to make a bigger batch in a larger unit, such as a 5-, 6-, or 7-quart **CROCK-POT®** slow cooker, the guidelines for doubling or tripling ingredients include:

● When preparing dishes with beef or pork in a larger unit, first browning the meat in a skillet yields the best results; the meat will cook more evenly.

● Roasted meats, chicken, and turkey quantities may be doubled or tripled, and seasonings adjusted by half. Caution: Flavorful spices such as garlic and chili powder will intensify during long slow cooking. Add more spices as desired (maybe 25 to 50 percent more) to balance the flavors.

● When preparing a soup or a stew, you may double all ingredients except liquids, seasonings, and dried herbs. Initially, increase liquid volume by half, or as needed. The **CROCK-POT®** slow cooker lid collects steam, which condenses to keep foods moist and to maintain liquid volume. Do not double thickeners, such as cornstarch, at the beginning. You may always add more thickener later if it's necessary.

Cooking Temperatures and Food Safety

Cooking meats in your **CROCK-POT®** slow cooker is perfectly safe. According to the U.S. Department of Agriculture, bacteria in food is killed at a temperature of 165°F. Meats cooked in the **CROCK-POT®** slow cooker reach an internal temperature of 170°F in beef and as high as 190°F in poultry. It's important to follow the recommended cooking times and to keep the cover on your **CROCK-POT®** slow cooker during cooking to maintain food-safe temperatures.

One-Step
DISHES

Easy Beef Burgundy

MAKES 4 TO 6 SERVINGS

PREP TIME: 10 minutes
COOK TIME: 6 to 8 hours (LOW)

1½ pounds beef round steak or beef stew meat, cut into 1-inch pieces

1 can (10¾ ounces) condensed cream of mushroom soup, undiluted

1 cup red wine

1 small onion, chopped

1 can (4 ounces) sliced mushrooms, drained

1 package (1 ounce) dry onion soup mix

1 tablespoon minced garlic

Combine all ingredients in **CROCK-POT®** slow cooker. Cover; cook on LOW 6 to 8 hours or until beef is tender.

Parmesan Potato Wedges

MAKES 6 SERVINGS | **PREP TIME:** 15 minutes
COOK TIME: 4 hours (HIGH)

2 pounds red potatoes, cut into ½-inch wedges
¼ cup finely chopped yellow onion
1½ teaspoons dried oregano
½ teaspoon salt
¼ teaspoon black pepper, or to taste
2 tablespoons butter, cut into ⅛-inch pieces
¼ cup (1 ounce) grated Parmesan cheese

Layer potatoes, onion, oregano, salt, pepper and butter in **CROCK-POT®** slow cooker. Cover; cook on HIGH 4 hours. Transfer potatoes to serving platter and sprinkle with cheese.

Chicken Teriyaki

MAKES 4 SERVINGS | **PREP TIME:** 10 minutes
COOK TIME: 2 hours (LOW)

1 pound boneless, skinless chicken tenders
1 can (6 ounces) pineapple juice
¼ cup soy sauce
1 tablespoon sugar
1 tablespoon minced fresh ginger
1 tablespoon minced garlic
1 tablespoon vegetable oil
1 tablespoon molasses
24 cherry tomatoes (optional)
2 cups hot cooked rice

Combine all ingredients except rice in **CROCK-POT®** slow cooker. Cover; cook on LOW 2 hours or until chicken is tender. Serve chicken and sauce over rice.

Parmesan Potato Wedges

Simple Slow Cooker Pork Roast

MAKES 6 SERVINGS | **PREP TIME:** 10 minutes
COOK TIME: 6 to 8 hours (LOW)

4 to 5 red potatoes, cut into bite-size pieces
4 carrots, cut into bite-size pieces
1 marinated pork loin roast* (3 to 4 pounds)
½ cup water
1 package (10 ounces) frozen baby peas
Salt and black pepper, to taste

*If marinated roast is unavailable, prepare marinade by mixing ¼ cup olive oil,
1 tablespoon minced garlic and 1½ tablespoons Italian seasoning. Place in large
resealable plastic food storage bag with pork roast. Marinate in refrigerator at least
2 hours or overnight.

Place potatoes, carrots and pork roast in **CROCK-POT®** slow cooker. (If
necessary, cut roast in half to fit.) Add water. Cover; cook on LOW 6 to 8 hours
or until vegetables are tender. Add peas during last hour of cooking. Transfer
pork to serving platter. Add salt and pepper, if desired. Slice and serve with
vegetables.

Green Bean Casserole

MAKES 4 TO 6 SERVINGS | **PREP TIME:** 10 minutes
COOK TIME: 3 to 4 hours (LOW)

2 packages (10 ounces each) frozen green beans, thawed
1 can (10¾ ounces) condensed cream of mushroom soup, undiluted
1 tablespoon chopped parsley
1 tablespoon chopped roasted red peppers
1 teaspoon dried sage
½ teaspoon salt
½ teaspoon black pepper
¼ teaspoon ground nutmeg
½ cup toasted slivered almonds

Combine all ingredients except almonds in **CROCK-POT®** slow cooker. Cover; cook on LOW 3 to 4 hours. Sprinkle with almonds before serving.

Nice 'n' Easy Italian Chicken

MAKES 4 SERVINGS | **PREP TIME:** 10 minutes
COOK TIME: 6 to 8 hours (LOW)

4 boneless, skinless chicken breasts (about 1 pound)
8 ounces mushrooms, sliced
1 medium green bell pepper, chopped
1 medium zucchini, diced
1 medium onion, chopped
1 jar (26 ounces) pasta sauce
Hot cooked linguini or spaghetti

Combine all ingredients except pasta in **CROCK-POT®** slow cooker. Cover; cook on LOW 6 to 8 hours or until chicken is tender. Serve over pasta.

Green Bean Casserole

Pumpkin-Cranberry Custard

MAKES 4 TO 6 SERVINGS | **PREP TIME:** 10 minutes
COOK TIME: 4 to 4½ hours (HIGH)

1 can (30 ounces) pumpkin pie filling
1 can (12 ounces) evaporated milk
1 cup dried cranberries
4 eggs, beaten
1 cup crushed or whole gingersnap cookies (optional)
  Whipped cream (optional)

Combine pumpkin, evaporated milk, cranberries and eggs in **CROCK-POT®** slow cooker; mix thoroughly. Cover; cook on HIGH 4 to 4½ hours. Serve with crushed or whole gingersnaps and whipped cream, if desired.

Polska Kielbasa with Beer & Onions

MAKES 6 TO 8 SERVINGS | **PREP TIME:** 10 minutes
COOK TIME: 4 to 5 hours (LOW)

⅓ cup honey mustard
⅓ cup packed dark brown sugar
18 ounces brown beer or ale
2 kielbasa sausages (16 ounces each), cut into 4-inch pieces
2 onions, quartered

Combine honey mustard and brown sugar in **CROCK-POT®** slow cooker. Whisk in beer. Add sausage pieces. Top with onions. Cover; cook on LOW 4 to 5 hours, stirring occasionally.

Pumpkin-Cranberry Custard

Chicken and Wild Rice Casserole

MAKES 4 TO 6 SERVINGS

PREP TIME: 15 minutes
COOK TIME: 3 to 4 hours (LOW)

  2 slices bacon, chopped
  3 tablespoons olive oil
1½ pounds chicken thighs, trimmed of excess skin
  ½ cup diced onion
  ½ cup diced celery
  2 tablespoons Worcestershire sauce
  ¾ teaspoon salt
  ¼ teaspoon black pepper
  ½ teaspoon dried sage
  1 cup converted long grain white rice
  1 package (4 ounces) wild rice
  6 ounces brown mushrooms, wiped clean and quartered*
  3 cups hot chicken broth, or enough to cover chicken
  2 tablespoons fresh chopped parsley (optional)

Use "baby bellas" or crimini mushrooms. Or, you may substitute white button mushrooms.

Microwave bacon on HIGH 1 minute. Transfer to **CROCK-POT®** slow cooker. Add olive oil and spread evenly on bottom. Place chicken in **CROCK-POT®** slow cooker, skin side down. Add onion, celery, Worcestershire sauce, salt, pepper, sage, white rice, wild rice, mushrooms and broth. Cover; cook on LOW 3 to 4 hours, or until rice is tender. Uncover and let stand 15 minutes. Garnish with chopped parsley, if desired.

Chicken Mozambique

MAKES 4 SERVINGS | **PREP TIME:** 10 minutes
COOK TIME: 8 hours (LOW) or
6 hours (HIGH)

2½ pounds boneless, skinless chicken breasts
1 cup white wine
½ cup (1 stick) butter, cut into small pieces
1 small onion, chopped
2 tablespoons minced garlic
2 tablespoons lemon juice
2 tablespoons hot pepper sauce
1 teaspoon salt
Hot cooked rice
Paprika (optional)

Place chicken, wine, butter, onion, garlic, lemon juice, pepper sauce and salt in **CROCK-POT®** slow cooker. Cover; cook on LOW 8 hours or on HIGH 6 hours. Serve chicken and sauce with rice. Sprinkle with paprika, if desired.

Rough-Cut Smoky Red Pork Roast

MAKES 8 SERVINGS | **PREP TIME:** 10 minutes
COOK TIME: 5 hours (HIGH)

1 pork shoulder roast (about 4 pounds)
1 can (about 14 ounces) stewed tomatoes, drained
1 can (6 ounces) tomato paste with basil, oregano and garlic
1 cup chopped red bell pepper
2 to 3 canned chipotle peppers in adobo sauce, finely chopped and mashed with fork*
1 teaspoon salt
1½ to 2 tablespoons sugar

For less heat, remove seeds from chipotle peppers before mashing.

Coat **CROCK-POT®** slow cooker with nonstick cooking spray. Place pork, fat side up, in bottom. Combine tomatoes, tomato paste, bell pepper and chipotle peppers in small bowl. Pour over pork. Cover; cook on HIGH 5 hours. Scrape tomato mixture into cooking liquid. Transfer pork to cutting board; let stand 15 minutes. Stir sugar into cooking liquid. Cook, uncovered, on HIGH 15 minutes longer. To serve, remove fat from pork and slice. Pour sauce over pork slices.

Hamburger Veggie Soup

MAKES 4 TO 6 SERVINGS | **PREP TIME:** 5 minutes
COOK TIME: 4 hours (HIGH)

1 pound 95% lean ground beef
1 bag (16 ounces) frozen mixed vegetables
1 package (10 ounces) frozen seasoning-blend vegetables
1 can (10¾ ounces) condensed tomato soup, undiluted
1 can (about 14 ounces) stewed tomatoes, undrained
2 cans (5½ ounces each) spicy vegetable juice
   Salt and black pepper, to taste

Coat **CROCK-POT®** slow cooker with nonstick cooking spray. Crumble beef before placing in bottom. Add remaining ingredients. Stir well to blend. Cover; cook on HIGH 4 hours. If necessary, break up large pieces of beef. Add salt and pepper before serving, if desired.

Smothered Beef Patties

MAKES 8 SERVINGS | **PREP TIME:** 10 minutes
COOK TIME: 8 hours (LOW)

   Worcestershire sauce, to taste
   Garlic powder, to taste
   Salt and black pepper, to taste
1 can (about 14 ounces) Mexican-style diced tomatoes with green
   chiles, undrained, divided
8 frozen beef patties, unthawed
1 onion, cut into 8 slices

Sprinkle bottom of **CROCK-POT®** slow cooker with small amount of Worcestershire sauce, garlic powder, salt, pepper and 2 tablespoons tomatoes with juice. Add 1 frozen beef patty. Top with small amount of Worcestershire, garlic powder, salt, pepper, 2 tablespoons tomatoes with juice and 1 onion slice. Repeat layers 7 times. Cover; cook on LOW 8 hours.

Hamburger Veggie Soup

Mexican Corn Bread Pudding

MAKES 8 SERVINGS | **PREP TIME:** 5 minutes
COOK TIME: 2 to 2½ hours (LOW)

1 can (14¾ ounces) cream-style corn
2 eggs
1 can (4 ounces) diced mild green chiles
2 tablespoons vegetable oil
¾ cup yellow cornmeal
2 tablespoons sugar
2 teaspoons baking powder
¾ teaspoon salt
½ cup shredded Cheddar cheese

Coat 2-quart **CROCK-POT®** slow cooker with nonstick cooking spray. Combine corn, eggs, chiles, oil, cornmeal, sugar, baking powder and salt in medium bowl. Stir well to blend. Pour into **CROCK-POT®** slow cooker. Cover; cook on LOW 2 to 2½ hours or until center is set. Sprinkle cheese over top. Cover and let stand 5 minutes or until cheese is melted.

Easy Beef Stroganoff

MAKES 4 TO 6 SERVINGS | **PREP TIME:** 5 minutes
COOK TIME: 6 hours (LOW) or
3 hours (HIGH)

3 cans (10¾ ounces each) condensed cream of mushroom soup, undiluted
1 cup sour cream
½ cup water
1 package (1 ounce) dry onion soup mix
2 pounds beef stew meat, cut into 1-inch pieces

Combine soup, sour cream, water and soup mix in **CROCK-POT®** slow cooker. Add beef; stir until well coated. Cover; cook on LOW 6 hours or on HIGH 3 hours.

Mexican Corn Bread Pudding

Creamy Chicken

MAKES 3 SERVINGS | **PREP TIME:** 5 minutes
COOK TIME: 6 to 8 hours (LOW)

3 boneless, skinless chicken breasts or 6 boneless, skinless chicken thighs
2 cans (10¾ ounces each) condensed cream of chicken soup, undiluted
1 can (about 14 ounces) chicken broth
1 can (4 ounces) sliced mushrooms, drained
½ medium onion, diced
Salt and black pepper, to taste

Place all ingredients except salt and pepper in **CROCK-POT®** slow cooker. Cover; cook on LOW 6 to 8 hours. Add salt and pepper, if desired.

Hungarian Lamb Goulash

MAKES 6 SERVINGS | **PREP TIME:** 10 minutes
COOK TIME: 6 to 8 hours (LOW)

1 package (16 ounces) frozen cut green beans, thawed
1 cup chopped onion
1¼ pounds lean lamb for stew, cut into 1-inch cubes
1 can (15 ounces) chunky tomato sauce
1¾ cups fat-free reduced-sodium chicken broth
1 can (6 ounces) tomato paste
4 teaspoons paprika
3 cups hot cooked egg noodles

Place green beans and onion in **CROCK-POT®** slow cooker. Top with lamb. Combine tomato sauce, broth, tomato paste and paprika in large bowl; mix well. Pour over lamb mixture. Cover; cook on LOW 6 to 8 hours. Stir goulash before serving over noodles.

Creamy Chicken

Meatless Sloppy Joes

MAKES 4 SERVINGS

PREP TIME: 15 minutes
COOK TIME: 5 to 5½ hours (LOW)

2 cups thinly sliced onions
2 cups chopped green bell peppers
1 can (about 15 ounces) kidney beans, drained and mashed
1 can (8 ounces) tomato sauce
2 tablespoons ketchup
1 tablespoon yellow mustard
2 cloves garlic, finely chopped
1 teaspoon chili powder
Cider vinegar (optional)
4 sandwich rolls

Combine onions, bell peppers, beans, tomato sauce, ketchup, mustard, garlic and chili powder in **CROCK-POT®** slow cooker. Cover; cook on LOW 5 to 5½ hours or until vegetables are tender. Season to taste with cider vinegar, if desired. Serve on rolls.

Arroz con Queso

MAKES 8 TO 10 SERVINGS | PREP TIME: 10 to 15 minutes
COOK TIME: 6 to 9 hours (LOW)

1 can (16 ounces) whole tomatoes, crushed
1 can (about 15 ounces) black beans, rinsed and drained
1½ cups uncooked converted long grain rice
1 onion, chopped
1 cup cottage cheese
1 can (4 ounces) chopped green chiles
2 tablespoons vegetable oil
3 teaspoons minced garlic
2 cups grated Monterey Jack cheese, divided

Combine tomatoes, beans, rice, onion, cottage cheese, chiles, oil, garlic and
1 cup Monterey Jack cheese in **CROCK-POT®** slow cooker; mix thoroughly.
Cover; cook on LOW 6 to 9 hours or until liquid is absorbed. Sprinkle with
remaining Monterey Jack cheese before serving.

4 INGREDIENTS or Less

PANTRY LOOKING BARE? PUT TOGETHER A GREAT
MEAL WITH JUST A FEW INGREDIENTS.

Chorizo Chili

MAKES 6 SERVINGS | **PREP TIME:** 5 minutes
COOK TIME: 7 hours (LOW)

1 pound 90% lean ground beef

8 ounces bulk raw chorizo sausage or ½ package (15 ounces) raw
chorizo sausage*

1 can (16 ounces) chili beans in chili sauce

2 cans (about 14 ounces each) zesty chili-style diced tomatoes,
undrained

*A highly seasoned Mexican pork sausage.

1. Place beef and chorizo in **CROCK-POT®** slow cooker. Break up with fork to
form small chunks.

2. Stir in beans and tomatoes and juice. Cover; cook on LOW 7 hours. Skim off
and discard excess fat before serving.

Bacon and Onion Brisket

MAKES 6 SERVINGS

PREP TIME: 20 minutes
COOK TIME: 6 to 8 hours (HIGH)

6 slices bacon, cut crosswise into ½-inch strips

1 flat-cut boneless beef brisket, seasoned with salt and black pepper (about 2½ pounds)

3 medium onions, sliced

2 cans (10½ ounces each) condensed beef consommé, undiluted

1. Cook bacon strips in large skillet over medium-high heat about 3 minutes. Do not overcook. Transfer bacon with slotted spoon to **CROCK-POT®** slow cooker.

2. Sear brisket in hot bacon fat on all sides, turning as it browns. Transfer to **CROCK-POT®** slow cooker.

3. Lower skillet heat to medium. Add sliced onions to skillet. Cook and stir 3 to 5 minutes or until softened. Add to **CROCK-POT®** slow cooker. Pour in consommé. Cover; cook on HIGH 6 to 8 hours or until meat is tender.

4. Transfer brisket to cutting board and let rest 10 minutes. Slice brisket against the grain into thin slices, and arrange on platter. Add salt and pepper, if desired. Spoon bacon, onions and cooking liquid over brisket to serve.

Easy Chocolate Pudding Cake

MAKES 16 SERVINGS | **PREP TIME:** 20 minutes
COOK TIME: 1½ hours (HIGH)

1 package (6-serving size) instant chocolate pudding and pie filling mix

3 cups milk

1 package (about 18 ounces) chocolate fudge cake mix, plus ingredients to prepare mix

Crushed peppermint candies (optional)

Whipped topping or ice cream (optional)

1. Coat 4-quart **CROCK-POT®** slow cooker with nonstick cooking spray. Place pudding mix in **CROCK-POT®** slow cooker. Whisk in milk.

2. Prepare cake mix according to package directions. Carefully pour cake mix into **CROCK-POT®** slow cooker. Do not stir. Cover; cook on HIGH 1½ hours or until cake tester inserted into center comes out clean.

3. Spoon into cups or onto plates; serve warm with crushed peppermint candies and whipped topping, if desired.

TIP: Allow breads, cakes and puddings to cool at least 5 minutes before scooping or removing them from the **CROCK-POT®** *slow cooker stoneware.*

Slow Cooker Turkey Breast

MAKES 4 TO 6 SERVINGS | **PREP TIME:** 5 minutes
COOK TIME: 6 to 8 hours (LOW) or
2½ to 3 hours (HIGH)

½ to 1 teaspoon garlic powder, or to taste
½ to 1 teaspoon paprika, or to taste
1 turkey breast (4 to 6 pounds)
1 tablespoon dried parsley flakes, or to taste

1. Blend garlic powder and paprika. Rub into turkey skin. Place turkey in **CROCK-POT®** slow cooker. Sprinkle on parsley. Cover; cook on LOW 6 to 8 hours or on HIGH 2½ to 3 hours or until internal temperature reaches 165°F when meat thermometer is inserted into thickest part of breast, not touching bone.

2. Transfer turkey to cutting board; cover with foil and let stand 10 to 15 minutes before carving. (Internal temperature will rise 5° to 10°F during stand time.)

Fantastic Pot Roast

MAKES 6 SERVINGS | **PREP TIME:** 5 minutes
COOK TIME: 6 to 8 hours (LOW)

1 can (12 ounces) cola
1 bottle (10 ounces) chili sauce
2 cloves garlic (optional)
2½ pounds boneless beef chuck roast

Combine cola, chili sauce and garlic, if desired, in **CROCK-POT®** slow cooker. Add beef, and turn to coat. Cover; cook on LOW 6 to 8 hours. Serve with sauce.

Chili and Cheese "Baked" Potato Supper

MAKES 4 SERVINGS | **PREP TIME:** 10 minutes
COOK TIME: 8 to 10 hours (LOW) or 4 to 5 hours (HIGH)

4 russet potatoes (about 2 pounds)
2 cups prepared chili
½ cup (2 ounces) shredded Cheddar cheese
4 tablespoons sour cream (optional)
2 green onions, sliced

1. Prick potatoes in several places with fork. Wrap potatoes in aluminum foil. Place in **CROCK-POT®** slow cooker. Cover; cook on LOW 8 to 10 hours or on HIGH 4 to 5 hours. Carefully unwrap potatoes and place on serving dish.

2. Heat chili in microwave or on stovetop. Split hot potatoes and spoon chili on top. Sprinkle with cheese, sour cream, if desired, and green onions.

Fantastic Pot Roast

Posole

MAKES 8 SERVINGS

PREP TIME: 10 minutes

COOK TIME: 5 hours (HIGH) or 10 hours (LOW)

3 pounds pork tenderloin, cubed
3 cans (about 14 ounces each) white hominy, drained
1 cup chili sauce

Combine all ingredients in **CROCK-POT®** slow cooker. Cover; cook on HIGH 5 hours or on LOW 10 hours.

Easy Family Burritos

MAKES 8 SERVINGS

PREP TIME: 5 minutes

COOK TIME: 9 to 11 hours (LOW)

1 boneless beef chuck shoulder roast (2 to 3 pounds)
1 jar (24 ounces) or 2 jars (16 ounces each) salsa
   Flour tortillas, warmed
   Optional toppings: shredded cheese, sour cream, salsa,
      shredded lettuce, diced tomato, diced onion or guacamole

1. Place roast in **CROCK-POT®** slow cooker; top with salsa. Cover; cook on LOW 8 to 10 hours.

2. Remove beef from **CROCK-POT®** slow cooker. Shred beef with two forks. Return to cooking liquid and mix well. Cover; cook 1 to 2 hours longer or until heated through.

3. Serve shredded beef wrapped in warm tortillas. Top as desired.

Posole

Cherry Delight

MAKES 8 TO 10 SERVINGS

PREP TIME: 10 minutes

COOK TIME: 3 to 4 hours (LOW) or
1½ to 2 hours (HIGH)

1 can (21 ounces) cherry pie filling
1 package (about 18 ounces) yellow cake mix
½ cup (1 stick) butter, melted
⅓ cup chopped walnuts
   Whipped topping or vanilla ice cream (optional)

1. Place pie filling in **CROCK-POT®** slow cooker. Mix together cake mix and butter in medium bowl. Spread evenly over pie filling. Sprinkle walnuts on top.

2. Cover; cook on LOW 3 to 4 hours or on HIGH 1½ to 2 hours. Spoon into serving dishes. Serve warm with whipped topping or ice cream, if desired.

Barbecue Roast Beef

MAKES 10 TO 12 SANDWICHES | **PREP TIME:** 5 minutes
COOK TIME: 2 hours (LOW)

2 pounds boneless cooked roast beef
1 bottle (12 ounces) barbecue sauce
1½ cups water
10 to 12 sandwich rolls, halved

1. Combine roast beef, barbecue sauce and water in **CROCK-POT®** slow cooker. Cover; cook on LOW 2 hours.

2. Remove beef from **CROCK-POT®** slow cooker. Shred with two forks. Return beef to sauce; mix well. Serve on rolls.

TIP: Freeze leftovers as individual portions; just reheat in a microwave for fast meals!

Glazed Pork Loin

MAKES 4 SERVINGS | **PREP TIME:** 5 minutes
COOK TIME: 8 hours (LOW) or
4 hours (HIGH)

1 bag (1 pound) baby carrots
4 boneless pork loin chops
1 jar (8 ounces) apricot preserves

Place carrots on bottom of **CROCK-POT®** slow cooker. Place pork on carrots; spread with preserves. Cover; cook on LOW 8 hours or on HIGH 4 hours.

Barbecue Roast Beef

Chicken and Biscuits

MAKES 4 SERVINGS | **PREP TIME:** 10 minutes
COOK TIME: 4½ hours (LOW)

4 boneless, skinless chicken breasts, cut into bite-size pieces
1 can (10¾ ounces) condensed cream of chicken soup
1 package (10 ounces) frozen peas and carrots
1 package (7½ ounces) refrigerated biscuits

1. Place chicken pieces in **CROCK-POT®** slow cooker. Pour soup over chicken. Cover; cook on LOW 4 hours or until chicken is tender and no longer pink in center.

2. Stir in frozen vegetables. Cover and cook 30 minutes longer until vegetables are heated through.

3. Bake biscuits according to package directions. Spoon chicken and vegetable mixture over biscuits and serve.

Harvest Ham Supper

MAKES 6 SERVINGS | **PREP TIME:** 15 minutes
COOK TIME: 6 to 8 hours (LOW)

6 carrots, cut into 2-inch pieces
3 medium sweet potatoes, quartered
1 to 1½ pounds boneless ham
1 cup maple syrup

1. Arrange carrots and potatoes in bottom of **CROCK-POT®** slow cooker.

2. Place ham on top of vegetables. Pour syrup over ham and vegetables. Cover; cook on LOW 6 to 8 hours.

Chicken and Biscuits

Triple Chocolate Fantasy

MAKES 36 PIECES | **PREP TIME:** 10 minutes
COOK TIME: 1 hour (HIGH) plus 1 hour (LOW)

2 pounds white almond bark, broken into pieces
1 bar (4 ounces) sweetened chocolate, broken into pieces*
1 package (12 ounces) semisweet chocolate chips
3 cups lightly toasted, coarsely chopped pecans**

Use your favorite high-quality chocolate candy bar.

**To toast pecans, spread in single layer on baking sheet. Bake in preheated 350°F oven 8 to 10 minutes or until golden brown, stirring frequently.*

1. Place bark, sweetened chocolate and chocolate chips in **CROCK-POT®** slow cooker. Cover; cook on HIGH 1 hour. Do not stir.

2. Turn **CROCK-POT®** slow cooker to LOW. Continue cooking 1 hour, stirring every 15 minutes. Stir in nuts.

3. Drop mixture by tablespoonfuls onto baking sheet covered with waxed paper; let cool. Store in tightly covered container.

VARIATIONS: Here are a few ideas for other imaginative items to add in along with or instead of pecans: raisins, crushed peppermint candy, candy-coated baking bits, crushed toffee, peanuts or pistachios, chopped gum drops, chopped dried fruit, candied cherries, chopped marshmallows or sweetened coconut.

Spicy Shredded Chicken

MAKES 6 SERVINGS | **PREP TIME:** 5 minutes
COOK TIME: 6 to 8 hours (LOW)

6 boneless, skinless chicken breasts (about 1½ pounds)
1 jar (16 ounces) salsa
  Flour tortillas, warmed
  Optional toppings: shredded cheese, sour cream, shredded
    lettuce, diced tomato, diced onion or sliced avocado

1. Place chicken in **CROCK-POT®** slow cooker. Cover with salsa. Cover; cook on LOW 6 to 8 hours or until chicken is tender and no longer pink in center.

2. Shred chicken with two forks. Serve with warmed tortillas and top as desired.

Cheesy Slow Cooker Potatoes

MAKES 6 SERVINGS | **PREP TIME:** 5 minutes
COOK TIME: 6 to 8 hours (LOW)

1 bag (32 ounces) shredded hash brown potatoes
2 cans (10¾ ounces each) condensed Cheddar cheese soup,
    undiluted
1 can (12 ounces) evaporated milk
1 cup chopped onion

Combine all ingredients in **CROCK-POT®** slow cooker. Cover; cook on LOW 6 to 8 hours.

Spicy Shredded Chicken

Italian Beef

MAKES 8 SERVINGS | **PREP TIME:** 5 minutes
COOK TIME: 10 hours (LOW)

1 beef rump roast (3 to 5 pounds)
1 can (about 14 ounces) beef broth
2 cups mild giardiniera
8 crusty Italian bread rolls, split

1. Place roast in **CROCK-POT®** slow cooker; add broth and giardiniera. Cover; cook on LOW 10 hours.

2. Remove beef from **CROCK-POT®** slow cooker. Shred beef with two forks. Return to cooking liquid; mix well. To serve, spoon beef and sauce onto rolls.

Orange Chicken

MAKES 4 SERVINGS | **PREP TIME:** 5 minutes
COOK TIME: 5 to 6 hours (LOW)

1 can (12 ounces) orange soda
½ cup soy sauce
4 boneless, skinless chicken breasts (about 1 pound)
Hot cooked rice

Pour soda and soy sauce into **CROCK-POT®** slow cooker. Add chicken and turn to coat. Cover; cook on LOW 5 to 6 hours. Serve over rice.

Italian Beef

Easy Cheesy BBQ Chicken

MAKES 6 SERVINGS | **PREP TIME:** 5 minutes
COOK TIME: 8 to 9 hours (LOW)

6 boneless, skinless chicken breasts (about 1½ pounds)
1 bottle (26 ounces) barbecue sauce
6 slices cooked bacon
6 slices Swiss cheese

1. Place chicken in **CROCK-POT®** slow cooker. Cover with barbecue sauce. Cover; cook on LOW 8 to 9 hours. (If sauce becomes too thick during cooking, add a little water.)

2. Before serving, cut bacon slices in half. Place 2 pieces cooked bacon on each chicken breast in **CROCK-POT®** slow cooker. Top each chicken breast with 1 slice cheese. Cover; cook on HIGH until cheese melts.

TIP: *To make cleanup easier, coat the inside of the* **CROCK-POT®** *slow cooker with nonstick cooking spray before adding the ingredients. To remove any sticky barbecue sauce residue, soak the stoneware in hot sudsy water, then scrub it with a plastic or nylon scrubber; don't use steel wool.*

Autumn Delight

MAKES 4 TO 6 SERVINGS

PREP TIME: 15 minutes
COOK TIME: 4 to 6 hours (LOW)

1 tablespoon olive oil

4 to 6 beef cubed steaks

2 cans (10¾ ounces each) condensed cream of mushroom soup, undiluted

1 cup water

1 package (1 ounce) dry onion soup mix or mushroom soup mix

1. Heat oil in large skillet over medium heat until hot. Lightly brown steaks on both sides. Transfer to **CROCK-POT®** slow cooker.

2. Combine soup, water and dry soup mix in large bowl; mix well. Pour over steaks. Cover; cook on LOW 4 to 6 hours.

Family
FAVORITES

Pizza Soup

MAKES 4 SERVINGS

PREP TIME: 10 minutes
COOK TIME: 6 to 7 hours (LOW)

2 cans (about 14 ounces each) stewed tomatoes with Italian seasonings, undrained
2 cups beef broth
1 cup sliced mushrooms
1 small onion, chopped
1 tablespoon tomato paste
¼ teaspoon salt, or to taste
¼ teaspoon black pepper, or to taste
½ pound turkey Italian sausage, casings removed
Shredded mozzarella cheese

1. Combine tomatoes with juice, broth, mushrooms, onion, tomato paste, salt and pepper in **CROCK-POT®** slow cooker.

2. Shape sausage into marble-size balls. Gently stir into soup mixture. Cover; cook on LOW 6 to 7 hours. Adjust salt and pepper, if necessary. Serve with cheese.

Pork Chops with Dried Fruit and Onions

MAKES 6 SERVINGS

PREP TIME: 20 minutes
COOK TIME: 3½ to 4 hours (LOW)

6 bone-in end-cut pork chops (about 2½ pounds)
Salt and black pepper, to taste
3 tablespoons vegetable oil
2 onions, diced
2 cloves garlic, minced
¼ teaspoon dried sage
¾ cup quartered pitted dried plums
¾ cup chopped mixed dried fruit
3 cups unsweetened unfiltered apple juice
1 bay leaf

1. Season pork chops with salt and pepper. Heat oil in large skillet over medium-high heat until hot. Sear pork on both sides to brown, cooking in batches, if necessary. Transfer to **CROCK-POT®** slow cooker.

2. Add onions to hot skillet. Reduce heat to medium; cook and stir until softened. Add garlic and cook 30 seconds more. Sprinkle sage over mixture. Add dried plums, mixed fruit and apple juice. Bring mixture to a boil. Reduce heat and simmer, uncovered, 3 minutes, scraping bottom and sides of pan to release browned bits. Ladle mixture over pork chops.

3. Add bay leaf. Cover; cook on LOW 3½ to 4 hours or until pork chops are tender. Remove and discard bay leaf. Add salt and pepper, if desired. To serve, spoon fruit and cooking liquid over pork chops.

Open-Face Provençal Vegetable Sandwich

MAKES 6 SERVINGS

PREP TIME: 15 minutes
COOK TIME: 5 to 6 hours (LOW)

2 cups sliced shiitake mushroom caps
1 large zucchini, halved lengthwise and sliced ¼ inch thick
1 large red bell pepper, cored, quartered lengthwise and thinly sliced
1 small onion, sliced lengthwise ¼ inch thick
1 small jalapeño pepper, cored, seeded and minced*
¼ cup vegetable or chicken broth
¼ cup pitted kalamata olives
2 tablespoons capers
1 clove garlic, minced
1½ tablespoons olive oil, divided
½ teaspoon crushed dried oregano
¼ teaspoon salt, or to taste
¼ teaspoon black pepper, or to taste
4 teaspoons white wine vinegar
Crusty bread, cut into thick slices
Shredded mozzarella cheese (optional)

Jalapeño peppers can sting and irritate the skin, so wear rubber gloves when handling peppers and do not touch your eyes.

1. Combine mushrooms, zucchini, bell pepper, onion, jalapeño, broth, olives, capers, garlic, 1 tablespoon oil, oregano, salt and black pepper in **CROCK-POT®** slow cooker. Cover; cook on LOW 5 to 6 hours.

2. Turn off **CROCK-POT®** slow cooker. Stir in vinegar and remaining ½ tablespoon oil. Let stand, uncovered, 15 to 30 minutes until vegetables absorb some of liquid. (Vegetable mixture should be lukewarm.) Add salt and pepper, if desired.

3. To serve, spoon onto bread. If desired, sprinkle each serving with 2 to 3 tablespoons shredded mozzarella cheese and broil 30 seconds, or until cheese melts and browns.

Chicken in Enchilada Sauce

MAKES 4 SERVINGS

PREP TIME: 10 minutes
COOK TIME: 6 to 7 hours (LOW)

1 can (about 14 ounces) diced tomatoes with chipotle chiles, undrained*

1 can (10 ounces) enchilada sauce

1 cup frozen or canned corn

¼ teaspoon ground cumin

¼ teaspoon black pepper, or to taste

1½ pounds boneless, skinless chicken thighs, cut into bite-size pieces

2 tablespoons minced fresh cilantro

½ cup shredded pepper jack cheese**

Sliced green onions (optional)

If tomatoes with chipotle chiles aren't available, use diced tomatoes with chiles or plain diced tomatoes plus ¼ teaspoon crushed red pepper flakes.

**For a less spicy dish, use Monterey Jack cheese.*

1. Combine tomatoes with juice, enchilada sauce, corn, cumin and pepper in **CROCK-POT®** slow cooker. Add chicken; mix well to combine. Cover; cook on LOW 6 to 7 hours.

2. Stir in cilantro. Spoon chicken and sauce into 4 bowls. Sprinkle each serving with 2 tablespoons cheese. Garnish with green onions.

Southwestern Salmon Po' Boys

MAKES 4 SERVINGS

PREP TIME: 10 minutes
COOK TIME: 1½ hours (HIGH)

1 red bell pepper, cored, seeded and sliced
1 green bell pepper, cored, seeded and sliced
1 onion, sliced
½ teaspoon zesty Southwest chipotle seasoning
¼ teaspoon salt
¼ teaspoon black pepper
4 salmon fillets (about 6 ounces each), rinsed and patted dry
¾ cup Italian dressing
¼ cup water
4 large French sandwich rolls, split or French bread cut into 6-inch
   pieces and split
   Chipotle mayonnaise, to taste*
   Fresh cilantro (optional)
½ lemon, cut into 4 wedges

If unavailable, combine ¼ cup mayonnaise with ½ teaspoon adobo sauce. Or substitute regular mayonnaise.

1. Coat **CROCK-POT®** slow cooker with nonstick cooking spray. Arrange half each of sliced bell peppers and onions in bottom.

2. Blend seasoning, salt and black pepper in small bowl. Season both sides of salmon. Place salmon on top of vegetables in **CROCK-POT®** slow cooker. Pour Italian dressing over salmon. Spread remaining bell peppers and onions over salmon. Add water. Cover; cook on HIGH 1½ hours.

3. Toast rolls, if desired. Spread tops with chipotle mayonnaise and garnish with cilantro. Spoon 1 to 2 tablespoons cooking liquid onto roll bottoms. Place warm fillet on each roll (remove skin first, if desired). Top with vegetable mixture and roll tops. Serve with lemon wedges.

Chicken and
Spicy Black Bean Tacos

MAKES 4 SERVINGS | **PREP TIME:** 10 minutes
COOK TIME: 1¾ hours (HIGH)

    1 can (about 15 ounces) black beans, rinsed and drained
    1 can (10 ounces) tomatoes with mild green chiles, drained
 1½ teaspoons chili powder
  ¾ teaspoon ground cumin
    1 tablespoon plus 1 teaspoon extra-virgin olive oil, divided
 12 ounces boneless, skinless chicken breasts
 12 crisp corn taco shells
    Optional toppings: shredded lettuce, diced tomatoes, shredded
      cheese, sour cream, sliced black olives

1. Coat **CROCK-POT®** slow cooker with nonstick cooking spray. Add beans and tomatoes with chiles. Blend chili powder and cumin with 1 teaspoon oil in small bowl; rub onto chicken breasts. Place chicken in **CROCK-POT®** slow cooker. Cover; cook on HIGH 1¾ hours.

2. Remove chicken and slice. Transfer bean mixture to bowl using slotted spoon. Stir in remaining 1 tablespoon oil.

3. To serve, warm taco shells according to package directions. Fill with equal amounts of bean mixture and chicken. Top as desired.

Hearty Chicken Chili

MAKES 6 SERVINGS | **PREP TIME:** 15 minutes
COOK TIME: 7 hours (LOW)

    1 medium onion, finely chopped
    1 small jalapeño pepper, cored, seeded and minced*
    1 small clove garlic, minced
 1½ teaspoons medium-hot chili powder
   ¾ teaspoon salt, or to taste
   ½ teaspoon black pepper, or to taste
   ½ teaspoon ground cumin
   ½ teaspoon crushed dried oregano
    2 cans (about 15 ounces each) hominy, rinsed and drained
    1 can (about 15 ounces) pinto beans, rinsed and drained
 1½ pounds boneless, skinless chicken thighs, cut into 1-inch pieces
    1 cup chicken broth
    1 tablespoon all-purpose flour (optional)
      Chopped fresh parsley or cilantro (optional)

Jalapeño peppers can sting and irritate the skin, so wear rubber gloves when handling peppers and do not touch your eyes. For a hotter dish, add ¼ teaspoon crushed red pepper flakes with the seasonings.

1. Combine onion, jalapeño, garlic, chili powder, salt, black pepper, cumin and oregano in **CROCK-POT®** slow cooker.

2. Add hominy, beans, chicken and broth. Stir well to combine. Cover; cook on LOW 7 hours.

3. If thicker gravy is desired, combine 1 tablespoon flour and 3 tablespoons cooking liquid in small bowl. Add to **CROCK-POT®** slow cooker. Cover; cook on HIGH 10 minutes or until thickened. Serve in bowls and garnish with parsley.

Cuban Pork Sandwiches

MAKES 8 SERVINGS

PREP TIME: 20 minutes

COOK TIME: 7 to 8 hours (LOW) or
3½ to 4 hours (HIGH)

   1 pork loin roast (about 2 pounds)

  ½ cup orange juice

   2 tablespoons lime juice

   1 tablespoon minced garlic

1½ teaspoons salt

  ½ teaspoon red pepper flakes

   8 crusty bread rolls, split in half (6 inches each)

   2 tablespoons yellow mustard

   8 slices Swiss cheese

   8 thin ham slices

   4 small dill pickles, thinly sliced lengthwise

1. Coat **CROCK-POT®** slow cooker with nonstick cooking spray. Add pork loin.

2. Combine orange juice, lime juice, garlic, salt and red pepper flakes in small bowl. Pour over pork. Cover; cook on LOW 7 to 8 hours or on HIGH 3½ to 4 hours. Transfer pork to cutting board and allow to cool. Cut into thin slices.

3. To serve, spread mustard on both sides of rolls. Divide pork slices among roll bottoms. Top each with Swiss cheese slice, ham slice and pickle slices; cover with top of roll.

4. Coat large skillet with nonstick cooking spray and heat over medium heat until hot. Working in batches, arrange sandwiches in skillet. Cover with foil and top with dinner plate to press down sandwiches. (If necessary, weigh down with 2 to 3 cans to compress sandwiches lightly.) Heat until cheese is slightly melted, about 8 minutes.* Serve immediately.

*Or use table top grill to compress and heat sandwiches.

Mock Piggies

MAKES 4 SERVINGS | PREP TIME: 20 minutes
COOK TIME: 8 hours (LOW)

1 head cabbage
1 pound 90% lean ground beef
1 cup cooked rice
1 onion, chopped
1 teaspoon salt
½ teaspoon black pepper
2 cans (10¾ ounces each) tomato soup
1 can water (measured in soup can)

1. Heat large saucepan of water to boiling point. Cut out core of cabbage. Place cabbage head into boiling water. Cook until leaves separate and are tender.

2. Meanwhile, place ground beef, rice, onion, salt and pepper in large bowl. Stir well to combine.

3. Line bottom of **CROCK-POT®** slow cooker with half of cabbage leaves. Place meat mixture on top.

4. Combine soup and water. Pour half of soup mixture over meat. Arrange remaining cabbage over meat to cover completely. Top with remaining soup. Cover; cook on LOW 8 hours.

Greek Chicken Pitas with Creamy Mustard Sauce

MAKES 4 SERVINGS | PREP TIME: 10 minutes
COOK TIME: 1¾ hours (HIGH)

Filling

1 medium green bell pepper, cored, seeded and sliced into ½-inch strips

1 medium onion, cut into 8 wedges

1 pound boneless, skinless chicken breasts, rinsed and patted dry

1 tablespoon extra-virgin olive oil

2 teaspoons dried Greek seasoning blend

¼ teaspoon salt

Sauce

¼ cup plain fat-free yogurt

¼ cup mayonnaise

1 tablespoon prepared mustard

¼ teaspoon salt

4 whole pita rounds

½ cup crumbled feta cheese

Optional toppings: sliced cucumbers, sliced tomatoes, kalamata olives

1. Coat **CROCK-POT®** slow cooker with nonstick cooking spray. Place bell pepper and onion in bottom. Add chicken, and drizzle with oil. Sprinkle evenly with Greek seasoning and ¼ teaspoon salt. Cover; cook on HIGH 1¾ hours or until chicken is no longer pink in center (vegetables will be slightly tender-crisp).

2. Remove chicken and slice. Remove vegetables using slotted spoon.

3. Combine yogurt, mayonnaise, mustard and ¼ teaspoon salt in small bowl. Whisk until smooth.

4. Warm pitas according to package directions. Cut in half, and layer with chicken, sauce, vegetables and feta cheese. Top as desired.

Spanish Chicken with Rice

MAKES 6 SERVINGS

PREP TIME: 20 minutes
COOK TIME: 3½ to 4 hours (HIGH)

2 tablespoons olive oil

11 ounces cooked linguiça or kielbasa sausage, sliced into ½-inch rounds

6 boneless, skinless chicken thighs (about 1 pound)

1 onion, diced

5 cloves garlic, minced

2 cups converted long grain white rice

½ cup diced carrots

1 red bell pepper, cored, seeded and diced

½ teaspoon salt

¼ teaspoon black pepper

¼ teaspoon saffron threads (optional)

3½ cups hot fat-free, reduced-sodium chicken broth

½ cup frozen peas, thawed

1. Heat oil in medium skillet over medium heat until hot. Add sausage and brown on both sides. Transfer to **CROCK-POT®** slow cooker with slotted spoon.

2. Add chicken to skillet and brown on all sides. Transfer to **CROCK-POT®** slow cooker. Add onion to skillet, and cook and stir until soft. Stir in garlic and cook 30 seconds longer. Transfer to **CROCK-POT®** slow cooker.

3. Add rice, carrots, bell pepper, salt, black pepper and saffron, if desired. Pour broth over mixture. Cover; cook on HIGH 3½ to 4 hours.

4. Before serving, stir in peas. Cook 15 minutes or until heated through.

Country Chicken and Vegetables with Creamy Herb Sauce

MAKES 4 SERVINGS

PREP TIME: 20 minutes
COOK TIME: 3½ hours (HIGH)

1 pound new potatoes, cut into ½-inch wedges
1 medium onion, cut into 8 wedges
½ cup coarsely chopped celery
4 bone-in chicken drumsticks, skinned
4 bone-in chicken thighs, skinned
1 can (10¾ ounces) cream of chicken soup
1 packet (1 ounce) ranch-style dressing mix
½ teaspoon dried thyme
¼ teaspoon black pepper, or to taste
½ cup heavy cream
   Salt, to taste
¼ cup finely chopped green onions (green and white parts)

1. Coat **CROCK-POT®** slow cooker with nonstick cooking spray. Arrange potatoes, onion and celery in bottom. Add chicken. Combine soup, dressing mix, thyme and pepper in small bowl. Spoon mixture evenly over chicken and vegetables. Cover; cook on HIGH 3½ hours.

2. Transfer chicken to shallow serving bowl with slotted spoon. Add cream and salt, if desired, to cooking liquid. Stir well to blend. Pour sauce over chicken. Garnish with green onions.

NOTE: To skin chicken easily, grasp skin with paper towel and pull away. Repeat with fresh paper towel for each piece of chicken, discarding skins and towels.

Best Beef Brisket Sandwich Ever

MAKES 10 TO 12 SERVINGS

PREP TIME: 15 minutes

COOK TIME: 10 hours (LOW)

1 beef brisket (about 3 pounds)

2 cups apple cider, divided

1 head garlic, cloves separated, crushed and peeled

2 tablespoons whole peppercorns

⅓ cup chopped fresh thyme *or* 2 tablespoons dried thyme

1 tablespoon mustard seeds

1 tablespoon Cajun seasoning

1 teaspoon ground allspice

1 teaspoon ground cumin

1 teaspoon celery seeds

2 to 4 whole cloves

1 bottle (12 ounces) dark beer

10 to 12 sourdough sandwich rolls, sliced in half

1. Place brisket, ½ cup cider, garlic, peppercorns, thyme, mustard seeds, Cajun seasoning, allspice, cumin, celery seeds and cloves in large resealable food storage bag. Seal bag; marinate in refrigerator overnight.

2. Place brisket and marinade in **CROCK-POT®** slow cooker. Add remaining 1½ cups cider and beer. Cover; cook on LOW 10 hours or until brisket is tender.

3. Slice brisket and place on sandwich rolls. Strain sauce; drizzle over meat.

*TIP: Unless you have a 5-, 6- or 7-quart **CROCK-POT®** slow cooker, cut any roast larger than 2½ pounds in half so it cooks completely.*

Honey Ribs

MAKES 4 SERVINGS

PREP TIME: 10 to 20 minutes

COOK TIME: 6 to 8 hours (LOW) or
4 to 6 hours (HIGH)

1 can (10¾ ounces) condensed beef consommé, undiluted
½ cup water
3 tablespoons soy sauce
2 tablespoons honey
2 tablespoons maple syrup
2 tablespoons barbecue sauce
½ teaspoon dry mustard
2 pounds pork baby back ribs, trimmed

1. Combine consommé, water, soy sauce, honey, syrup, barbecue sauce and mustard in **CROCK-POT®** slow cooker; mix well.

2. Cut ribs into 3- to 4-rib portions. Transfer to **CROCK-POT®** slow cooker. (If ribs are especially fatty, broil 10 minutes before adding.) Cover; cook on LOW 6 to 8 hours or on HIGH 4 to 6 hours or until ribs are tender.

3. Cut into individual ribs. Serve with sauce.

Ham and Cheese Pasta Bake

MAKES 6 SERVINGS | PREP TIME: 15 minutes
COOK TIME: 3½ to 4 hours (LOW)

6 cups water
2 teaspoons salt
12 ounces uncooked rigatoni
1 ham steak, cubed
1 container (10 ounces) refrigerated light Alfredo sauce
2 cups mozzarella cheese, divided
2 cups half-and-half, warmed
1 tablespoon cornstarch

1. Bring water to a boil in medium saucepan. Stir in salt. Add rigatoni and boil 7 minutes. Drain well and transfer to **CROCK-POT®** slow cooker.

2. Stir in ham, Alfredo sauce and 1 cup mozzarella cheese. Whisk together half-and-half and cornstarch in small bowl. Pour half-and-half mixture over pasta to cover. Sprinkle with remaining cheese. Cover; cook on LOW 3½ to 4 hours. (Dish is done when rigatoni is tender and excess liquid is absorbed.)

Scalloped Potatoes and Ham

MAKES 5 TO 6 SERVINGS | PREP TIME: 20 minutes
COOK TIME: 3½ hours (HIGH) plus
1 hour (LOW)

6 large russet potatoes, sliced into ¼-inch rounds
1 ham steak (about 1½ pounds), cut into cubes
1 can (10¾ ounces) condensed cream of mushroom soup, undiluted
1 soup can water
1 cup (about 4 ounces) shredded Cheddar cheese
Grill seasoning, to taste

1. Coat **CROCK-POT®** slow cooker with nonstick cooking spray. Arrange potatoes and ham in layers in **CROCK-POT®** slow cooker.

2. Combine soup, water, cheese and grill seasoning in medium bowl; pour over potatoes and ham. Cover; cook on HIGH about 3½ hours or until potatoes are fork-tender. Turn heat to LOW and cook 1 hour.

Backroads Ham and Potato Casserole

MAKES 4 TO 6 SERVINGS | PREP TIME: 15 minutes
COOK TIME: 3 to 5 hours (HIGH)

2 pounds baking potatoes, cut into 1-inch cubes
½ teaspoon dried thyme
12 ounces cubed ham
1 can (10¾ ounces) condensed cream of chicken soup, undiluted
4 ounces cream cheese, cut into ½-inch cubes
½ cup finely chopped green onions
½ cup frozen peas, thawed

1. Coat **CROCK-POT®** slow cooker with nonstick cooking spray. Place potatoes in bottom. Add thyme and ham. Spread soup evenly over potatoes and ham. Cover; cook on HIGH 3 to 5 hours.

2. Gently stir in cream cheese, green onions and peas. Cover; cook 5 minutes longer or until cheese is melted.

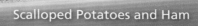
Scalloped Potatoes and Ham

Sloppy Sloppy Joes

MAKES 20 TO 25 SERVINGS | PREP TIME: 30 minutes
COOK TIME: 4 to 6 hours (LOW)

    4 pounds ground beef
    1 cup chopped onion
    1 cup chopped green bell pepper
    1 can (about 28 ounces) tomato sauce
    2 cans (10¾ ounces each) condensed tomato soup, undiluted
    1 cup packed brown sugar
    ¼ cup ketchup
    3 tablespoons Worcestershire sauce
    1 tablespoon ground mustard
    1 tablespoon prepared mustard
 1½ teaspoons chili powder
    1 teaspoon garlic powder
      Toasted sandwich rolls or hamburger buns

1. Brown beef in large skillet over medium-high heat, stirring to break up meat. Drain and discard fat.

2. Add onion and bell pepper; cook and stir 5 to 10 minutes or until onion is translucent and mixture is fragrant.

3. Transfer mixture to **CROCK-POT®** slow cooker. Add tomato sauce, soup, brown sugar, ketchup, Worcesterhshire sauce, ground mustard, prepared mustard, chili powder and garlic powder; stir until well blended. Cover; cook on LOW 4 to 6 hours. Serve on rolls.

Slow Cooker Cheese Soup

MAKES 4 SERVINGS

PREP TIME: 10 minutes
COOK TIME: 2 to 3 hours (LOW)

2 cans (10¾ ounces each) condensed cream of celery soup, undiluted
4 cups (16 ounces) shredded Cheddar cheese
1 teaspoon paprika
1 teaspoon Worcestershire sauce
1¼ cups half-and-half
Salt and black pepper, to taste

1. Combine soup, cheese, paprika and Worcestershire sauce in **CROCK-POT®** slow cooker.

2. Cover; cook on LOW 2 to 3 hours.

3. Add half-and-half; stir until blended. Cover; cook another 20 minutes. Season to taste with salt and pepper.

TIP: Turn simple soup into a super supper by serving it in individual bread bowls. Cut a small slice from the tops of small, round loaves of a hearty bread (such as Italian or sourdough), and remove the insides, leaving a 1½-inch shell. Pour in soup and serve.

Comforting
CLASSICS

HAVE EVERYONE'S FAVORITE MEAL READY
FOR SIT-DOWN SUPPERS

Easy Beef Stew

MAKES 6 TO 8 SERVINGS | **PREP TIME:** 15 minutes
COOK TIME: 8 to 10 hours (LOW)

1½ to 2 pounds beef stew meat, cut into 1-inch cubes

4 medium potatoes, cut into 1-inch cubes

4 carrots, cut into 1½-inch pieces *or*
    4 cups baby carrots

1 medium onion, cut into 8 wedges

2 cans (8 ounces each) tomato sauce

1 teaspoon salt

½ teaspoon black pepper

Chopped parsley, for garnish

Combine all ingredients in **CROCK-POT®** slow cooker. Cover; cook on LOW 8 to 10 hours or until vegetables are tender. Garnish as desired.

Zesty Chicken and Rice Supper

MAKES 3 TO 4 SERVINGS | **PREP TIME:** 10 minutes
COOK TIME: 6 to 8 hours (LOW) or
3 to 4 hours (HIGH)

2 boneless, skinless chicken breasts, cut into 1-inch pieces
2 large green bell peppers, coarsely chopped
1 small onion, chopped
1 can (about 28 ounces) diced tomatoes, undrained
1 cup uncooked converted long grain white rice
1 cup water
1 package (about 1 ounce) taco seasoning
1 teaspoon salt
1 teaspoon black pepper
1 teaspoon ground red pepper
Shredded Cheddar cheese (optional)

Place all ingredients except cheese in **CROCK-POT®** slow cooker. Stir well to combine. Cover; cook on LOW 6 to 8 hours or on HIGH 3 to 4 hours. Garnish with cheese.

Sweet and Sour Chicken

MAKES 4 SERVINGS | **PREP TIME:** 10 minutes
COOK TIME: 2½ to 3½ hours (LOW)

¼ cup chicken broth
2 tablespoons low-sodium soy sauce
2 tablespoons hoisin sauce
1 tablespoon cider vinegar
1 tablespoon tomato paste
2 teaspoons packed brown sugar
1 clove garlic, minced
¼ teaspoon black pepper
1 pound boneless, skinless chicken thighs, cut into 1-inch pieces
2 teaspoons cornstarch
2 tablespoons snipped fresh chives
Hot cooked rice

1. Combine broth, soy sauce, hoisin sauce, vinegar, tomato paste, brown sugar, garlic and pepper in **CROCK-POT®** slow cooker. Stir well to mix.

2. Add chicken thighs; stir well to coat. Cover; cook on LOW 2½ to 3½ hours.

3. Remove chicken with slotted spoon; keep warm. Combine cornstarch and 2 tablespoons cooking liquid in small bowl. Add to **CROCK-POT®** slow cooker. Stir in chives. Turn heat to HIGH. Stir 2 minutes or until sauce is slightly thickened. Serve chicken and sauce over rice.

Asian Beef with Broccoli

MAKES 4 TO 6 SERVINGS

PREP TIME: 15 minutes
COOK TIME: 3 hours (HIGH)

1½ pounds boneless beef chuck steak (about 1½ inches thick) sliced into thin strips*

1 can (10½ ounces) condensed beef consommé, undiluted

½ cup oyster sauce

2 tablespoons cornstarch

1 bag (16 ounces) fresh broccoli florets

Hot cooked rice

Sesame seeds (optional)

*To make slicing steak easier, place in freezer for 30 minutes to firm up.

1. Place beef in **CROCK-POT®** slow cooker. Pour consommé and oyster sauce over beef. Cover; cook on HIGH 3 hours.

2. Combine cornstarch and 2 tablespoons cooking liquid in small bowl. Add to **CROCK-POT®** slow cooker. Stir well to combine. Cover; cook on HIGH 15 minutes longer or until thickened.

3. Poke holes in broccoli bag with fork. Microwave on HIGH 3 minutes. Empty bag into **CROCK-POT®** slow cooker. Gently toss beef and broccoli together. Serve over cooked rice. Garnish with sesame seeds.

Creamy Chicken and Spinach Lasagna

MAKES 4 SERVINGS | **PREP TIME:** 20 minutes
COOK TIME: 3 hours (LOW)

1¼ cups shredded Swiss or mozzarella cheese, divided
1 cup ricotta cheese
1 teaspoon dried oregano
¼ teaspoon red pepper flakes
1 container (10 ounces) refrigerated Alfredo pasta sauce
⅓ cup water
4 no-boil lasagna noodles
1 package (10 ounces) frozen chopped spinach, thawed and squeezed dry
1½ cups cooked diced chicken
¼ cup grated Parmesan cheese
Red pepper flakes (optional)

1. Combine 1 cup Swiss cheese, ricotta, oregano and ¼ teaspoon red pepper flakes in small bowl; set aside. Blend Alfredo sauce with water; set aside.

2. Coat **CROCK-POT®** slow cooker with nonstick cooking spray. Break 2 lasagna noodles in half and place on bottom. Spread half of ricotta mixture over noodles. Top with half of spinach. Arrange half of chicken and half of Parmesan over spinach. Pour half of Alfredo mixture over top. Repeat layers, beginning with noodles and ending with Alfredo mixture. Cover; cook on LOW 3 hours.

3. Sprinkle remaining ¼ cup Swiss cheese on top. Cover and let stand 5 minutes or until cheese is melted. To serve, cut into squares or wedges. Garnish with red pepper flakes.

Slow-Cooked Beef Brisket Dinner

MAKES 8 TO 10 SERVINGS

PREP TIME: 15 minutes
COOK TIME: 6 to 8 hours (LOW)

1 beef brisket (4 pounds), cut in half
4 to 6 medium potatoes, cut into large chunks
6 carrots, cut into 1-inch pieces
8 ounces mushrooms, sliced
½ large onion, sliced
1 stalk celery, cut into 1-inch pieces
3 cubes beef bouillon
5 cloves garlic, crushed
1 teaspoon black peppercorns
2 bay leaves
  Water, as needed
  Salt and black pepper, to taste
  Chopped fresh parsley (optional)

1. Place brisket, potatoes, carrots, mushrooms, onion, celery, bouillon cubes, garlic, peppercorns and bay leaves in **CROCK-POT®** slow cooker. Add enough water to cover ingredients. Cover; cook on LOW 6 to 8 hours.

2. Remove and discard bay leaves. Transfer brisket to cutting board. Season with salt and pepper to taste. Slice meat across grain. Serve with vegetables. Garnish with parsley.

Spicy Grits with Chicken

MAKES 6 SERVINGS | **PREP TIME:** 10 minutes
COOK TIME: 4 hours (LOW)

4 cups chicken broth

1 cup grits*

1 jalapeño pepper, cored, seeded and finely chopped**

½ teaspoon salt, or to taste

¼ teaspoon paprika

¼ teaspoon black pepper, or to taste

¾ cup shredded sharp Cheddar cheese

1½ cups chopped cooked chicken breast (about 12 ounces total)

½ cup half-and-half

2 tablespoons chopped fresh chives, plus additional for garnish

Use coarse, instant, yellow or stone-ground grits.

**Jalapeño peppers can sting and irritate the skin, so wear rubber gloves when handling peppers and do not touch your eyes.*

1. Combine broth, grits, jalapeño, salt, paprika and black pepper in **CROCK-POT®** slow cooker. Stir well. Cover; cook on LOW 4 hours. (Consistency of cooked grits should be like cream of wheat.)

2. Add cheese and stir until melted. Stir in chicken, half-and-half and 2 tablespoons chives. Add salt and pepper, if desired. Cover; cook on LOW 15 minutes to blend flavors. Garnish with additional chives, if desired. Serve immediately.

No-Fuss Macaroni & Cheese

MAKES 6 TO 8 SERVINGS

PREP TIME: 10 minutes
COOK TIME: 2 to 3 hours (LOW)

2 cups (about 8 ounces) uncooked elbow macaroni
4 ounces light pasteurized processed cheese, cubed
1 cup (4 ounces) shredded mild Cheddar cheese
½ teaspoon salt
⅛ teaspoon black pepper
1½ cups fat-free (skim) milk

Combine macaroni, cheeses, salt and pepper in **CROCK-POT®** slow cooker. Pour milk over all. Cover; cook on LOW 2 to 3 hours, stirring after 20 to 30 minutes.

Baked Beans

MAKES 6 TO 8 SERVINGS

PREP TIME: 10 minutes
COOK TIME: 8 to 12 hours (LOW) or
3 to 4 hours (HIGH)

2 cans (16 ounces each) baked beans
1 cup ketchup
½ cup barbecue sauce
½ cup packed brown sugar
5 slices bacon, chopped
½ green bell pepper, chopped
½ onion, chopped
1½ teaspoons prepared mustard
Fresh parsley (optional)

Place all ingredients in **CROCK-POT®** slow cooker. Stir well to combine. Cover; cook on LOW 8 to 12 hours or on HIGH 3 to 4 hours. Garnish with fresh parsley.

No-Fuss Macaroni & Cheese

Classic Pot Roast

MAKES 6 TO 8 SERVINGS | **PREP TIME:** 30 minutes
COOK TIME: 8 to 10 hours (LOW)

1 tablespoon vegetable oil
1 beef chuck shoulder roast (3 to 4 pounds)
6 medium potatoes, halved
6 carrots, sliced
2 onions, quartered
2 stalks celery, sliced
1 can (about 14 ounces) diced tomatoes, undrained
Salt and black pepper
Dried oregano
Water
1½ to 2 tablespoons all-purpose flour

1. Heat oil in large skillet over medium-low heat. Add roast; brown on all sides. Transfer to **CROCK-POT®** slow cooker.

2. Add potatoes, carrots, onions, celery and tomatoes with juice. Season with salt, pepper and oregano. Add enough water to cover bottom of **CROCK-POT®** slow cooker by about ½ inch. Cover; cook on LOW 8 to 10 hours. Remove roast to platter. Let stand 15 minutes.

3. Transfer juices to small saucepan. Whisk in flour until smooth. Cook and stir over medium heat until thickened. Slice roast and serve with gravy.

Meatballs and Spaghetti Sauce

MAKES 6 TO 8 SERVINGS

PREP TIME: 20 minutes
COOK TIME: 3 to 5 hours (LOW) or
2 to 4 hours (HIGH)

Meatballs

2 pounds 90% lean ground beef
1 cup bread crumbs
1 onion, chopped
2 eggs, beaten
¼ cup minced fresh Italian parsley
2 teaspoons minced garlic
½ teaspoon dry mustard
½ teaspoon black pepper
Olive oil

Spaghetti Sauce

1 can (28 ounces) peeled whole tomatoes
½ cup chopped fresh basil
2 tablespoons olive oil
2 cloves garlic, or to taste, finely minced
1 teaspoon sugar
Salt and black pepper, to taste

Cooked spaghetti

1. Combine all meatball ingredients except oil. Form into walnut-sized balls. Heat oil in skillet over medium heat until hot. Sear meatballs on all sides, turning as they brown. Transfer to **CROCK-POT®** slow cooker.

2. Combine all sauce ingredients in medium bowl. Pour over meatballs, stirring to coat. Cover; cook on LOW 3 to 5 hours or on HIGH 2 to 4 hours.

3. Adjust seasonings, if desired. Serve over spaghetti.

TIP: Recipe can be doubled for a 5-, 6- or 7-quart **CROCK-POT®** *slow cooker.*

Campfired-Up Sloppy Joes

MAKES 6 SERVINGS | **PREP TIME:** 20 minutes
COOK TIME: 3 hours (HIGH)

1½ pounds lean ground beef
½ cup chopped sweet onion
1 medium red bell pepper, cored, seeded and chopped
1 large clove garlic, crushed
½ cup ketchup
½ cup barbecue sauce
2 tablespoons cider vinegar
1 tablespoon Worcestershire sauce
1 tablespoon packed brown sugar
1 teaspoon chili powder
1 can (8 ounces) baked beans
6 kaiser rolls, split and warmed
Shredded sharp Cheddar cheese (optional)

1. Brown ground beef, onion, bell pepper and garlic 6 to 8 minutes in large skillet over medium-high heat, stirring to break up meat. Drain and discard excess fat. Transfer beef mixture to **CROCK-POT®** slow cooker.

2. Combine ketchup, barbecue sauce, vinegar, Worcestershire sauce, brown sugar and chili powder in small bowl. Transfer to **CROCK-POT®** slow cooker.

3. Add beans. Stir well to combine. Cover; cook on HIGH 3 hours.

4. To serve, fill split rolls with ½ cup sloppy joe mixture. Sprinkle with Cheddar cheese, if desired, before topping sandwich with roll lid.

SERVING SUGGESTION: Serve with a side of coleslaw.

Slow Cooker Chicken Dinner

MAKES 4 SERVINGS | **PREP TIME:** 5 minutes
COOK TIME: 6 to 8 hours (LOW)

4 boneless, skinless chicken breasts (about 1 pound)
1 can (10¾ ounces) condensed cream of chicken soup, undiluted
⅓ cup milk
1 package (6 ounces) stuffing mix
1⅔ cups water

1. Place chicken in **CROCK-POT®** slow cooker. Combine soup and milk in small bowl; mix well. Pour soup mixture over chicken.

2. Combine stuffing mix and water. Spoon stuffing over chicken. Cover; cook on LOW 6 to 8 hours.

My Favorite Chicken

MAKES 4 SERVINGS | **PREP TIME:** 15 minutes
COOK TIME: 6 to 8 hours (LOW)

1 whole chicken (about 3 pounds), cut into pieces
1 cup chopped onion
1 cup sliced celery
1 cup sliced carrots
½ teaspoon seasoned salt
½ teaspoon black pepper
¼ teaspoon garlic powder
¼ teaspoon poultry seasoning
3 to 4 medium potatoes, cut into slices
1 can (about 14 ounces) chicken broth

Place chicken, onion, celery, carrots, seasoned salt, pepper, garlic powder and poultry seasoning in **CROCK-POT®** slow cooker. Top with potatoes. Add broth. Cover; cook on LOW 6 to 8 hours.

Slow Cooker Chicken Dinner

Super Easy
Chicken Noodle Soup

MAKES 4 SERVINGS | **PREP TIME:** 15 minutes
COOK TIME: 5 to 7 hours (LOW) or
3 to 4 hours (HIGH)

1 can (about 48 ounces) chicken broth
2 boneless, skinless chicken breasts, cut into bite-size pieces
4 cups water
⅔ cup diced onion
⅔ cup diced celery
⅔ cup diced carrots
⅔ cup sliced mushrooms
½ cup frozen peas
4 chicken bouillon cubes
2 tablespoons butter
1 tablespoon dried parsley flakes
1 teaspoon salt
1 teaspoon ground cumin
1 teaspoon dried marjoram
1 teaspoon black pepper
2 cups cooked egg noodles

Combine all ingredients except noodles in **CROCK-POT®** slow cooker. Cover; cook on LOW 5 to 7 hours or on HIGH 3 to 4 hours. Stir in noodles 30 minutes before serving.

Barbecued Pulled Pork Sandwiches

MAKES 8 SERVINGS

PREP TIME: 15 to 20 minutes
COOK TIME: 11 to 13 hours (LOW) or 6 to 7 hours (HIGH)

1 pork shoulder roast (2½ pounds)
1 bottle (14 ounces) barbecue sauce
1 tablespoon fresh lemon juice
1 teaspoon packed brown sugar
1 medium onion, chopped
8 sandwich rolls or hamburger buns

1. Place pork roast in **CROCK-POT®** slow cooker. Cover; cook on LOW 10 to 12 hours or on HIGH 5 to 6 hours.

2. Remove pork roast from **CROCK-POT®**. Shred with two forks. Discard cooking liquid. Return pork to **CROCK-POT®**; add barbecue sauce, lemon juice, brown sugar and onion. Cover and cook on LOW 2 hours or on HIGH 1 hour. Serve pork on rolls or buns.

NOTE: This kid-popular dish is sweet and savory, and most importantly, extremely easy to make. Serve with crunchy coleslaw on the side.

TIP: For a 5-, 6- or 7-quart **CROCK-POT®** slow cooker, double all ingredients except for the barbecue sauce. Increase the barbecue sauce to 1½ bottles (about 21 ounces total).

Curry Chicken with Peaches and Raisins

MAKES 2 SERVINGS | **PREP TIME:** 15 minutes
COOK TIME: 5 hours (LOW) or 3 to 3½ hours (HIGH)

2 peaches, peeled and sliced into ¼-inch slices, reserving 8 slices for garnish

Lemon juice

4 boneless, skinless chicken thighs *or* 2 boneless, skinless chicken breasts

Salt and black pepper, to taste

1 tablespoon olive oil

⅓ cup raisins, chopped*

1 shallot, thinly sliced

1 tablespoon grated fresh ginger

2 cloves garlic, crushed

½ teaspoon curry powder

1 teaspoon ground cumin

½ teaspoon whole cloves

¼ cup chicken stock

1 tablespoon cider vinegar

¼ teaspoon ground red pepper (optional)

1 teaspoon cornstarch (optional)

Fresh cilantro leaves (optional)

Hot cooked rice (optional)

Substitute ⅓ cup currants for chopped raisins.

1. Toss reserved slices of peaches with lemon juice to coat and refrigerate. Rinse, dry and season chicken with salt and black pepper.

2. Heat oil in skillet until hot. Add chicken and lightly brown, about 3 minutes per side. Transfer to **CROCK-POT®** slow cooker. Top with remaining peaches, raisins and shallot.

3. Whisk together ginger, garlic, curry powder, cumin, cloves, stock, vinegar

and ground red pepper, if desired. Pour mixture over chicken. Cover; cook on LOW 5 hours or on HIGH 3 to 3½ hours.

4. Transfer chicken to serving dish. Stir cornstarch into sauce to thicken, if desired. Spoon peaches, raisins and sauce over chicken. Top with reserved peaches and cilantro, if desired. Serve over rice, if desired.

Fall-Apart Pork Roast with Mole

MAKES 6 SERVINGS

PREP TIME: 10 to 15 minutes
COOK TIME: 7 to 8 hours (LOW) or
3 to 4 hours (HIGH)

⅔ cup whole almonds
⅔ cup raisins
3 tablespoons vegetable oil, divided
½ cup chopped onion
4 cloves garlic, chopped
2¾ pounds lean boneless pork shoulder roast, well trimmed
1 can (about 14 ounces) diced fire-roasted tomatoes or diced tomatoes, undrained
1 cup cubed bread, any variety
½ cup chicken broth
2 ounces Mexican chocolate, chopped
2 tablespoons chipotle peppers in adobo sauce, chopped
1 teaspoon salt
Fresh cilantro, coarsely chopped (optional)

1. Heat large skillet over medium-high heat until hot. Add almonds and toast 3 to 4 minutes, stirring frequently, until fragrant. Add raisins. Cook 1 to 2 minutes longer, stirring constantly, until raisins begin to plump. Place half of almond mixture in large mixing bowl. Reserve remaining half for garnish.

2. In same skillet, heat 1 tablespoon oil. Add onion and garlic. Cook and stir 2 to 3 minutes until softened. Add to almond mixture; set aside.

3. Heat remaining oil in same skillet. Add pork roast and brown on all sides, about 5 to 7 minutes. Transfer to **CROCK-POT®** slow cooker.

4. Combine tomatoes with juice, bread, broth, chocolate, chipotle peppers and salt with almond mixture. Purée mixture in blender, in 2 to 3 batches, until smooth. Pour purée over pork roast in **CROCK-POT®** slow cooker. Cover; cook on LOW 7 to 8 hours or on HIGH 3 to 4 hours or until pork is done.

5. Remove pork roast from **CROCK-POT®** slow cooker. Whisk sauce until smooth before spooning over pork roast. Garnish with reserved almond mixture and chopped cilantro.

Super
SOUPS & STEWS

BRING OUT THE BOWLS AND ENJOY
A HEARTY LUNCH OR DINNER

Irish Stew

MAKES 6 SERVINGS

PREP TIME: 10 minutes
COOK TIME: 7 to 9 hours (LOW)

1 cup fat-free reduced-sodium chicken broth
1 teaspoon dried marjoram
1 teaspoon dried parsley flakes
¾ teaspoon salt
½ teaspoon garlic powder
¼ teaspoon black pepper
1¼ pounds white potatoes, peeled and cut into 1-inch pieces
1 pound lean lamb for stew, cut into 1-inch cubes
8 ounces frozen cut green beans, thawed
2 small leeks, cut lengthwise into halves, then crosswise into slices
1½ cups coarsely chopped carrots

1. Combine broth, marjoram, parsley, salt, garlic powder and pepper in **CROCK-POT®** slow cooker; mix well.

2. Layer potatoes, lamb, green beans, leeks and carrots into **CROCK-POT®** slow cooker. Cover; cook on LOW 7 to 9 hours or until lamb is tender.

TIP: If desired, thicken cooking liquid with a mixture of 1 tablespoon cornstarch and ¼ cup water. Stir mixture into cooking liquid; cook on HIGH 10 to 15 minutes or until thickened.

Mexican Chicken and Black Bean Soup

MAKES 4 SERVINGS

PREP TIME: 10 minutes
COOK TIME: 3 to 4 hours (HIGH)

4 bone-in chicken thighs, skinned
1 cup finely chopped onion
1 can (about 14 ounces) fat-free chicken broth
1 can (about 14 ounces) diced tomatoes with Mexican seasoning
    or diced tomatoes with green chiles, undrained
1 can (about 15 ounces) black beans, rinsed and drained
1 cup frozen corn
1 can (4 ounces) chopped mild green chiles
1 tablespoon chili powder
1 teaspoon ground cumin
1 teaspoon salt, or to taste
    Optional toppings: sour cream, sliced avocado, shredded
        cheese, chopped cilantro, fried tortilla strips

1. Coat **CROCK-POT®** slow cooker with nonstick cooking spray. Add all ingredients except toppings. Cover; cook on HIGH 3 to 4 hours or until chicken is done.

2. Remove chicken with slotted spoon. Debone and chop chicken. Return to **CROCK-POT®** slow cooker and stir well. Serve in bowls. Top as desired.

NOTE: To skin chicken easily, grasp skin with paper towel and pull away. Repeat with fresh paper towel for each piece of chicken, discarding skins and towels.

Creamy Farmhouse Chicken and Garden Soup

MAKES 4 SERVINGS | **PREP TIME:** 15 minutes
COOK TIME: 3 to 4 hours (HIGH)

½ package (16 ounces) frozen pepper stir-fry vegetable mix
1 cup frozen corn
1 medium zucchini, sliced
2 bone-in chicken thighs, skinned
½ teaspoon minced garlic
1 can (about 14 ounces) fat-free chicken broth
½ teaspoon dried thyme
2 ounces uncooked egg noodles
1 cup half-and-half
½ cup frozen peas, thawed
2 tablespoons finely chopped fresh parsley
2 tablespoons butter
1 teaspoon salt
½ teaspoon coarsely ground black pepper

1. Coat **CROCK-POT®** slow cooker with nonstick cooking spray. Place stir-fry vegetables, corn and zucchini in bottom. Add chicken, garlic, broth and thyme. Cover; cook on HIGH 3 to 4 hours or until chicken is no longer pink in center. Remove chicken and set aside to cool slightly.

2. Add noodles to **CROCK-POT®** slow cooker. Cover; cook 20 minutes longer or until noodles are done.

3. Meanwhile, debone and chop chicken. Return to **CROCK-POT®** slow cooker. Stir in remaining ingredients. Let stand 5 minutes before serving.

NOTE: To skin chicken easily, grasp skin with paper towel and pull away. Repeat with fresh paper towel for each piece of chicken, discarding skins and towels.

Italian Sausage Soup

MAKES 4 TO 6 SERVINGS

PREP TIME: 15 minutes
COOK TIME: 5 to 6 hours (LOW)

Sausage Meatballs

    1 pound mild Italian sausage, casings removed

    ½ cup dried bread crumbs

    ¼ cup grated Parmesan cheese

    ¼ cup milk

    1 egg

    ½ teaspoon dried basil

    ½ teaspoon black pepper

    ¼ teaspoon garlic salt

Soup

    4 cups hot chicken broth

    1 tablespoon tomato paste

    1 clove garlic, minced

    ¼ teaspoon red pepper flakes

    ½ cup uncooked mini pasta shells*

    1 bag (10 ounces) baby spinach leaves

    Grated Parmesan cheese

Or use other tiny pasta, such as ditalini (mini tubes) or farfallini (mini bowties).

1. Combine all meatball ingredients. Roll into marble-size balls.

2. Combine broth, tomato paste, garlic and red pepper flakes in **CROCK-POT®** slow cooker. Add meatballs. Cover; cook on LOW 5 to 6 hours.

3. Thirty minutes before serving, add pasta. When pasta is tender, stir in spinach leaves. Ladle into bowls and sprinkle with Parmesan cheese. Serve immediately.

Curried Sweet Potato and Carrot Soup

MAKES 8 SERVINGS

PREP TIME: 10 minutes
COOK TIME: 7 to 8 hours (LOW)

2 medium-to-large sweet potatoes, peeled and cut into ¾-inch dice (about 5 cups)

2 cups baby carrots

1 small onion, chopped

¾ teaspoon curry powder

½ teaspoon salt, or to taste

½ teaspoon black pepper, or to taste

½ teaspoon ground cinnamon

¼ teaspoon ground ginger

4 cups chicken broth

1 tablespoon maple syrup

¾ cup half-and-half

Candied ginger (optional)

1. Place sweet potatoes, carrots, onion, curry powder, salt, pepper, cinnamon and ground ginger in **CROCK-POT**® slow cooker. Add broth. Stir well to combine. Cover; cook on LOW 7 to 8 hours.

2. Pureé soup, 1 cup at a time, in blender, returning blended soup to **CROCK-POT**® slow cooker after each batch. (Or, use immersion blender.) Add syrup and half-and-half. Add salt and pepper, if desired. Cover; cook on HIGH 15 minutes to reheat. Serve in bowls and garnish with strips or pieces of candied ginger.

TIP: For richer flavor, add a teaspoon of chicken soup base along with broth.

Sweet and Sour Brisket Stew

MAKES 6 TO 8 SERVINGS

PREP TIME: 10 minutes

COOK TIME: 8 hours (LOW)

1 jar (12 ounces) chili sauce

1½ to 2 tablespoons packed dark brown sugar

1½ tablespoons fresh lemon juice

¼ cup beef broth

1 tablespoon Dijon mustard

¼ teaspoon paprika

½ teaspoon salt, or to taste

¼ teaspoon black pepper, or to taste

1 clove garlic, minced

1 small onion, chopped

1 well-trimmed beef brisket, cut into 1-inch pieces*

2 large carrots, cut into ½-inch slices

1 tablespoon all-purpose flour (optional)

Beef brisket has a thick layer of fat, which some supermarkets trim off. If the meat is well trimmed, buy 2½ pounds; if not, purchase 4 pounds, then trim and discard excess fat.

1. Combine chili sauce, 1½ tablespoons brown sugar, lemon juice, broth, mustard, paprika, salt and pepper in **CROCK-POT®** slow cooker. (Add remaining sugar, if desired, after tasting.)

2. Add garlic, onion, beef and carrots. Stir well to coat. Cover; cook on LOW 8 hours.

3. If thicker gravy is desired, combine 1 tablespoon flour and 3 tablespoons cooking liquid in small bowl. Add to **CROCK-POT®** slow cooker. Cover; cook on HIGH 10 minutes or until thickened.

Smoked Sausage and Navy Bean Soup

MAKES 8 SERVINGS | **PREP TIME:** 15 minutes
COOK TIME: 8 to 9 hours (HIGH)

8 cups chicken broth

1 pound dried navy beans, sorted and rinsed

2 ham hocks (about 1 pound total)

2 onions, diced

1 cup diced carrots

1 cup diced celery

1 can (about 14 ounces) diced tomatoes, undrained

2 tablespoons tomato paste

2 cloves garlic, minced

1 bay leaf

1 teaspoon dried thyme

1 smoked sausage (1 pound), cut into ½-inch rounds

1. Bring broth to a boil in large saucepan over medium-high heat. Cover; reduce heat to low.

2. Place beans in **CROCK-POT®** slow cooker. Add ham hocks, onions, carrots, celery, tomatoes, tomato paste, garlic, bay leaf and thyme. Carefully pour in hot broth. Cover; cook on HIGH 8 to 9 hours or until beans are tender.

3. Remove and discard bay leaf. Remove ham hocks from **CROCK-POT®** slow cooker; let stand until cool enough to handle. Remove ham from hocks, chop and return to **CROCK-POT®** slow cooker. Stir in sausage. Cover; cook 15 to 30 minutes or until sausage is heated through.

Mushroom Barley Stew

MAKES 4 TO 6 SERVINGS

PREP TIME: 15 minutes
COOK TIME: 6 to 7 hours (LOW)

1 tablespoon olive oil
1 medium onion, finely chopped
1 cup chopped carrots (about 2 carrots)
1 clove garlic, minced
1 cup uncooked pearl barley
1 cup dried wild mushrooms, broken into pieces
1 teaspoon salt
½ teaspoon black pepper
½ teaspoon dried thyme
5 cups vegetable broth

1. Heat oil in medium skillet over medium-high heat. Add onion, carrots and garlic; cook and stir 5 minutes or until tender. Place in **CROCK-POT®** slow cooker.

2. Add barley, mushrooms, salt, pepper and thyme. Stir in broth. Cover; cook on LOW 6 to 7 hours. Adjust seasonings.

TIP: To turn this thick, robust stew into a soup, add 2 to 3 additional cups of broth. Cook the same length of time.

Panama Pork Stew

MAKES 6 SERVINGS | **PREP TIME:** 15 minutes
COOK TIME: 7 to 9 hours (LOW)

2 small sweet potatoes (about ¾ pound), peeled and cut into
    2-inch pieces
1 package (10 ounces) frozen corn
1 package (9 ounces) frozen cut green beans
1 cup chopped onion
1¼ pounds pork stew meat, cut into 1-inch cubes
1 can (about 14 ounces) diced tomatoes, undrained
¼ cup water
1 to 2 tablespoons chili powder
½ teaspoon salt
½ teaspoon ground coriander

1. Place potatoes, corn, green beans and onion in **CROCK-POT®** slow cooker. Top with pork.

2. Combine tomatoes with juice, water, chili powder, salt and coriander in medium bowl. Pour over pork. Cover; cook on LOW 7 to 9 hours.

Chicken Fiesta Soup

MAKES 8 SERVINGS | **PREP TIME:** 20 to 30 minutes
COOK TIME: 8 hours (LOW)

4 boneless, skinless chicken breasts, cooked and shredded
1 can (about 14 ounces) stewed tomatoes, drained
2 cans (4 ounces each) chopped green chiles
1 can (28 ounces) enchilada sauce
1 can (about 14 ounces) chicken broth
1 cup finely chopped onion
2 cloves garlic, minced
1 teaspoon ground cumin
1 teaspoon chili powder
1 teaspoon salt
¾ teaspoon black pepper
¼ cup finely chopped fresh cilantro
1 cup frozen whole kernel corn
1 yellow squash, diced
1 zucchini, diced
8 tostada shells, crumbled
8 ounces shredded Cheddar cheese

1. Combine chicken, tomatoes, chiles, enchilada sauce, broth, onion, garlic, cumin, chili powder, salt, pepper, cilantro, corn, squash and zucchini, in **CROCK-POT®** slow cooker.

2. Cover; cook on LOW 8 hours. Ladle soup into bowls; garnish with crumbled tostada shells and cheese.

Cioppino

MAKES 6 SERVINGS

PREP TIME: 20 to 30 minutes
COOK TIME: 10 to 12 hours (LOW),
plus 30 minutes (HIGH)

1 pound cod, halibut or any firm white fish, cubed
1 cup sliced mushrooms
2 carrots, sliced
1 onion, chopped
1 green bell pepper, chopped
1 teaspoon minced garlic
1 can (15 ounces) tomato sauce
1 can (about 14 ounces) beef broth
1 teaspoon salt
½ teaspoon black pepper
½ teaspoon dried oregano
1 can (7 ounces) cooked clams
½ pound cooked shrimp
1 package (6 ounces) cooked crabmeat
Minced fresh parsley

1. Combine fish pieces, mushrooms, carrots, onion, bell pepper, garlic, tomato sauce, broth, salt, black pepper and oregano in **CROCK-POT®** slow cooker. Cover; cook on LOW 10 to 12 hours.

2. Turn **CROCK-POT®** slow cooker to HIGH. Add clams, shrimp and crabmeat. Cover; cook on HIGH 30 minutes or until seafood is heated through. Garnish with parsley before serving.

Creamy Cauliflower Bisque

MAKES 9 SERVINGS | **PREP TIME:** 20 minutes
COOK TIME: 8 hours (LOW) or
4 hours (HIGH)

1 pound frozen cauliflower florets
1 pound baking potatoes, peeled and cut into 1-inch cubes
1 cup chopped yellow onion
2 cans (about 14 ounces each) chicken broth
½ teaspoon dried thyme
¼ teaspoon garlic powder
⅛ teaspoon ground red pepper
1 cup evaporated skim milk
2 tablespoons butter
½ teaspoon salt
¼ teaspoon black pepper
1 cup (4 ounces) shredded reduced-fat sharp Cheddar cheese
¼ cup finely chopped fresh parsley
¼ cup finely chopped green onions

1. Combine cauliflower, potatoes, onion, broth, thyme, garlic powder and ground red pepper in **CROCK-POT®** slow cooker. Cover; cook on LOW 8 hours, or on HIGH 4 hours.

2. Pour soup in blender in batches; process until smooth, holding lid down firmly. Return puréed batches to **CROCK-POT®** slow cooker. Add evaporated milk, butter, salt and black pepper; stir until blended.

3. Top individual servings with cheese, parsley and green onions.

Clam Chowder

MAKES 10 SERVINGS | **PREP TIME:** 10 minutes
COOK TIME: 3 to 4 hours (LOW)

5 cans (10¾ ounces each) condensed reduced-fat cream of potato soup, undiluted
2 cans (12 ounces each) evaporated skim milk
2 cans (10 ounces each) whole baby clams, rinsed and drained
1 can (14¾ ounces) cream-style corn
2 cans (4 ounces each) tiny shrimp, rinsed and drained
¾ cup crisp-cooked and crumbled bacon (about ½ pound)
　Lemon-pepper seasoning, to taste
　Oyster crackers

Combine all ingredients except crackers in **CROCK-POT®** slow cooker. Cover; cook on LOW 3 to 4 hours, stirring occasionally. Serve with oyster crackers.

NOTE: Chowder is a milk- or cream-based soup closely associated with New England. It's most often made with clams, but lobster and cod are other favored seafood ingredients.

Peppery Potato Soup

MAKES 6 SERVINGS | **PREP TIME:** 15 minutes
COOK TIME: 7 to 8½ hours (LOW)

2 cans (about 14 ounces each) chicken broth
4 small baking potatoes, halved and sliced crosswise
1 large onion, quartered and sliced
1 stalk celery, sliced
½ teaspoon salt
½ teaspoon black pepper
1 cup half-and-half
¼ cup all-purpose flour
1 tablespoon butter
   Celery leaves and fresh parsley (optional)

1. Combine broth, potatoes, onion, celery, salt and pepper in **CROCK-POT®** slow cooker; mix well. Cover; cook on LOW 6 to 7 hours.

2. Stir half-and-half into flour; stir mixture into **CROCK-POT®** slow cooker. Cover; cook on LOW 1 hour.

3. Slightly mash potato mixture with potato masher. Cook, uncovered, on LOW 30 minutes or until slightly thickened. Just before serving, stir in butter. Garnish with celery leaves and parsley.

Minestrone Alla Milanese

MAKES 8 TO 10 SERVINGS | **PREP TIME:** 20 minutes
COOK TIME: 6 to 7 hours (LOW)

2 cans (about 14 ounces each) reduced-sodium beef broth
1 can (about 14 ounces) diced tomatoes, undrained
1 cup diced red potatoes
1 cup coarsely chopped carrots
1 cup coarsely chopped green cabbage
1 cup sliced zucchini
¾ cup chopped onion
¾ cup sliced fresh green beans
¾ cup coarsely chopped celery
¾ cup water
2 tablespoons olive oil
1 clove garlic, minced
½ teaspoon dried basil
¼ teaspoon dried rosemary
1 bay leaf
1 can (about 15 ounces) cannellini beans, rinsed and drained
Grated Parmesan cheese (optional)

1. Combine all ingredients except cannellini beans and cheese in **CROCK-POT®** slow cooker; mix well. Cover; cook on LOW 5 to 6 hours.

2. Add cannellini beans. Cover; cook on LOW 1 hour or until vegetables are tender.

3. Remove and discard bay leaf before serving. Garnish with cheese.

Cherry Rice Pudding

MAKES 6 SERVINGS | **PREP TIME:** 10 minutes
COOK TIME: 4 to 5 hours (LOW)

1½ cups milk
1 cup hot cooked rice
3 eggs, beaten
½ cup sugar
¼ cup dried cherries or cranberries
½ teaspoon almond extract
¼ teaspoon salt
Ground nutmeg (optional)

1. Combine milk, rice, eggs, sugar, cherries, almond extract and salt in large bowl. Pour into greased 1½-quart casserole dish. Cover dish with buttered aluminum foil, butter side down.

2. Place rack in **CROCK-POT®** slow cooker and pour in 1 cup water. Place casserole on rack. Cover; cook on LOW 4 to 5 hours.

3. Remove casserole from **CROCK-POT®** slow cooker. Let stand 15 minutes before serving. Garnish with nutmeg.

Pepperoni Pizza Dip with Breadstick Dippers

MAKES 8 SERVINGS

PREP TIME: 20 minutes

COOK TIME: 2 hours (LOW) or
1 to 1½ hours (HIGH)

1 jar or can (14 ounces) pizza sauce
¾ cup chopped turkey pepperoni
4 green onions, chopped
1 can (2¼ ounces) sliced black olives, drained
½ teaspoon dried oregano
1 cup (4 ounces) shredded mozzarella cheese
1 package (3 ounces) cream cheese, softened
    Breadstick Dippers (recipe follows)

1. Combine pizza sauce, pepperoni, green onions, olives and oregano in 2-quart **CROCK-POT®** slow cooker. Cover; cook on LOW 2 hours or on HIGH 1 to 1½ hours or until mixture is hot.

2. Stir in mozzarella and cream cheese until melted and well blended. Serve with warm Breadstick Dippers.

Breadstick Dippers

1 package (8 ounces) refrigerated breadstick dough
2 teaspoons melted butter
2 teaspoons minced fresh Italian parsley

Bake breadsticks according to package directions. Brush with melted butter and sprinkle with parsley. Serve with warm dip.

Shrimp Louisiana-Style

MAKES 3 TO 4 SERVINGS

PREP TIME: 5 minutes
COOK TIME: 1¼ hours (HIGH)

1 pound shrimp, unpeeled, rinsed
½ cup (1 stick) butter, diced
⅓ cup lemon juice
1 tablespoon Worcestershire sauce
1 teaspoon minced garlic
1 teaspoon seafood seasoning
½ teaspoon salt
½ teaspoon coarsely ground black pepper
1½ teaspoons grated lemon peel, plus additional for garnish
Hot cooked rice (optional)
4 lemon wedges (optional)

1. Coat **CROCK-POT®** slow cooker with nonstick cooking spray. Place shrimp in bottom. Add butter, lemon juice, Worcestershire sauce, garlic, seafood seasoning, salt and pepper. Stir well to combine. Cover; cook on HIGH 1¼ hours.

2. Turn off **CROCK-POT®** slow cooker. Stir in 1½ teaspoons lemon peel. Let stand, uncovered, 5 minutes. Serve in shallow soup bowls over rice, if desired. Garnish with grated lemon peel and serve with lemon wedge.

Hot Tropics Sipper

MAKES 8 SERVINGS

PREP TIME: 5 minutes
COOK TIME: 3½ to 4 hours (HIGH)

4 cups pineapple juice
2 cups apple juice
1 container (about 11 ounces) apricot nectar
3 whole cinnamon sticks
6 whole cloves
½ cup packed dark brown sugar
1 medium lemon, thinly sliced
1 medium orange, thinly sliced
   Additional lemon or orange slices (optional)

Place pineapple juice, apple juice, apricot nectar, cinnamon, cloves, brown sugar, lemon and orange in **CROCK-POT®** slow cooker. Cover; cook on HIGH 3½ to 4 hours or until very fragrant. Strain immediately (beverage will turn bitter if fruit and spices remain after cooking is complete). Serve with fresh lemon or orange slices.

Spicy Sweet & Sour Cocktail Franks

MAKES ABOUT 4 DOZEN | PREP TIME: 5 minutes
COOK TIME: 2 to 3 hours (LOW)

2 packages (8 ounces each) cocktail franks
½ cup ketchup or chili sauce
½ cup apricot preserves
1 teaspoon hot pepper sauce
Additional hot pepper sauce (optional)

1. Combine all ingredients in 1½-quart **CROCK-POT®** slow cooker; mix well. Cover; cook on LOW 2 to 3 hours.

2. Serve warm or at room temperature with additional hot pepper sauce, if desired.

Angel Wings

MAKES 10 APPETIZERS | PREP TIME: 5 minutes
COOK TIME: 5 to 6 hours (LOW)

1 can (10¾ ounces) condensed tomato soup, undiluted
¾ cup water
¼ cup packed light brown sugar
2½ tablespoons balsamic vinegar
2 tablespoons chopped shallots
10 chicken wings

1. Combine soup, water, brown sugar, vinegar and shallots in **CROCK-POT®** slow cooker; mix well.

2. Add chicken wings; stir to coat with sauce. Cover; cook on LOW 5 to 6 hours or until cooked through and glazed with sauce.

*TIP: Don't use the **CROCK-POT®** slow cooker to reheat leftover foods. Transfer cooled leftovers to an airtight container and refrigerate. Use a microwave oven, a stove top or an oven for reheating.*

Spicy Sweet & Sour
Cocktail Franks

Chicken Cordon Bleu

MAKES 4 SERVINGS

PREP TIME: 20 minutes
COOK TIME: 2¼ hours (LOW)

¼ cup all-purpose flour
1 teaspoon paprika
½ teaspoon salt
¼ teaspoon black pepper
4 boneless chicken breasts (about 1 pound), lightly pounded*
4 slices ham
4 slices Swiss cheese
2 tablespoons olive oil
½ cup white cooking wine
½ cup chicken broth
½ cup half-and-half
2 tablespoons cornstarch

*Place chicken between two pieces of plastic food wrap and flatten with back of skillet.

1. Combine flour, paprika, salt and pepper in resealable plastic food storage bag and shake well; set aside.

2. Place flattened chicken on cutting board, skin side down. Place 1 slice ham and 1 slice cheese on each piece. Fold chicken up to enclose filling, and secure with toothpick. Place in bag with seasoned flour, and shake gently to coat.

3. Heat oil in large skillet over medium-high heat until hot. Add chicken, skin side down. Brown on all sides. Transfer to **CROCK-POT®** slow cooker.

4. Remove skillet from heat and add wine. Cook and stir to loosen browned bits. Pour into **CROCK-POT®** slow cooker. Add broth. Cover; cook on LOW 2 hours.

5. Remove chicken with slotted spoon. Cover with aluminum foil to keep warm. Mix together half-and-half and cornstarch. Add to cooking liquid. Cover, cook on LOW 15 minutes longer or until sauce has thickened. To serve, remove toothpicks, place chicken on plates and spoon sauce around chicken. Serve extra sauce on side.

Asian Barbecue Skewers

MAKES 4 TO 6 SERVINGS

PREP TIME: 10 minutes
COOK TIME: 3 hours (LOW)

2 pounds boneless, skinless chicken thighs
½ cup soy sauce
⅓ cup packed brown sugar
2 tablespoons sesame oil
3 cloves garlic, minced
½ cup thinly sliced green onions (optional)
1 tablespoon toasted sesame seeds (optional)

1. Cut each thigh into 4 pieces about 1½ inches thick. Thread chicken onto 7-inch-long wooden skewers, folding thinner pieces, if necessary. Place skewers into **CROCK-POT®** slow cooker, layering as flat as possible.

2. Combine soy sauce, brown sugar, oil and garlic in small bowl. Reserve ⅓ cup sauce; set aside. Pour remaining sauce over skewers. Cover; cook on LOW 2 hours. Turn skewers over and cook 1 hour longer.

3. Transfer skewers to serving platter. Discard cooking liquid. Spoon on reserved sauce and sprinkle with onions and sesame seeds, if desired.

Chocolate Hazelnut Pudding Cake

MAKES 10 SERVINGS

PREP TIME: 5 minutes
COOK TIME: 2½ hours (HIGH)

1 box (about 18 ounces) golden yellow cake mix
1 cup water
4 eggs
½ cup sour cream
½ cup vegetable oil
1 cup mini semisweet chocolate chips
½ cup chopped hazelnuts
    Whipped cream or ice cream (optional)

1. Coat 6-quart **CROCK-POT®** slow cooker with nonstick cooking spray. Combine cake mix, water, eggs, sour cream and oil; mix smooth. Pour batter into **CROCK-POT®** slow cooker. Cover; cook on HIGH 2 hours or until batter is nearly set.

2. Sprinkle on mini chocolate chips and hazelnuts. Cover; cook on HIGH 30 minutes longer or until toothpick inserted into center comes out clean or cake begins to pull away from sides of **CROCK-POT®** slow cooker. Let stand until cool and slice, or spoon out while warm. Serve with whipped cream, if desired.

Turkey Breast with Sweet Cranberry-Soy Sauce

MAKES 8 SERVINGS

PREP TIME: 10 minutes
COOK TIME: 3½ hours (HIGH)

1 bone-in turkey breast (6 to 7 pounds), thawed, rinsed and patted dry*
1 can (16 ounces) whole berry cranberry sauce
1 packet (1 ounce) dry onion soup mix
Grated peel and juice of 1 medium orange
3 tablespoons soy sauce
2 to 3 tablespoons cornstarch
1 to 1½ tablespoons sugar
1 to 1½ teaspoons cider vinegar
Salt, to taste

Substitute 2 (3½-pound) bone-in turkey breast halves, if necessary.

1. Coat **CROCK-POT®** slow cooker with nonstick cooking spray. Place turkey in bottom, meat side up. Combine cranberry sauce, soup mix, orange peel and orange juice in small bowl. Pour over turkey. Cover; cook on HIGH 3½ hours.

2. Scrape cranberry mixture into cooking liquid. Transfer turkey to cutting board. Let stand 15 minutes before slicing.

3. Combine soy sauce and cornstarch in small bowl. Stir into cooking liquid with sugar, vinegar and salt, if desired. Cover; cook on HIGH 15 minutes longer, or until thickened slightly. Serve sauce over sliced turkey.

Artichoke and Nacho Cheese Dip

MAKES ABOUT 1 QUART

PREP TIME: 5 minutes
COOK TIME: 2 hours (LOW)

2 cans (10¾ ounces each) condensed nacho cheese soup, undiluted

1 can (14 ounces) quartered artichoke hearts, drained and coarsely chopped

1 cup (4 ounces) shredded or thinly sliced pepper jack cheese

1 can (4 ounces) evaporated milk

2 tablespoons snipped fresh chives, divided

½ teaspoon paprika

Crackers or chips

1. Combine soup, artichoke hearts, cheese, evaporated milk, 1 tablespoon chives and paprika in **CROCK-POT®** slow cooker. Cover; cook on LOW 2 hours.

2. Stir well. Sprinkle with remaining 1 tablespoon chives and serve with crackers.

Apple Crumble Pot

MAKES 6 TO 8 SERVINGS | PREP TIME: 15 minutes
COOK TIME: 2¼ hours (HIGH)

Filling

⅔ cup packed dark brown sugar

2 tablespoons biscuit baking mix

1½ teaspoons ground cinnamon

¼ teaspoon ground allspice

½ cup dried cranberries

2 tablespoons butter, cubed

1 teaspoon vanilla

4 Granny Smith apples (about 2 pounds), cored and cut into 8 wedges each

Topping

1 cup prepared baking mix

½ cup rolled oats

⅓ cup packed dark brown sugar

3 tablespoons cold butter, cubed

½ cup chopped pecans

1. Coat **CROCK-POT®** slow cooker with nonstick cooking spray. Combine ⅔ cup brown sugar, 2 tablespoons baking mix, cinnamon and allspice in large bowl. Add remaining filling ingredients, and toss gently to coat evenly. Transfer to **CROCK-POT®** slow cooker.

2. Combine 1 cup baking mix, oats and ⅓ cup brown sugar in same large bowl. Cut in 3 tablespoons butter with pastry blender or two knives until mixture resembles pea-sized crumbs. Sprinkle evenly over filling in **CROCK-POT®** slow cooker. Top with pecans. Cover; cook on HIGH 2¼ hours or until apples are tender. Do not overcook.

3. Turn off **CROCK-POT®** slow cooker. Uncover and let stand 15 to 30 minutes before serving. Garnish as desired.

Spicy Orange Chicken Nuggets

MAKES 8 OR 9 SERVINGS

PREP TIME: 15 minutes
COOK TIME: 3 to 3½ hours (LOW)

    1 bag (28 ounces) frozen popcorn chicken bites
 1½ cups prepared honey teriyaki marinade
  ¾ cup orange juice concentrate
  ⅔ cup water
    1 tablespoon orange marmalade
  ¾ teaspoon hot chile sauce or sriracha*
      Thinly sliced green onions (optional)
      Hot cooked rice

Sriracha is a Thai hot sauce, and is available in Asian specialty markets.

1. Preheat oven to 450°F. Spread chicken evenly on baking sheet. Bake 12 to 14 minutes or until crisp. (Do not brown.) Transfer to **CROCK-POT®** slow cooker.

2. Combine teriyaki marinade, juice concentrate, water, marmalade and chile sauce in medium bowl. Pour over chicken. Cover; cook on LOW 3 to 3½ hours.

3. Sprinkle with onions and serve with rice.

Parmesan Ranch Snack Mix

MAKES ABOUT 9½ CUPS SNACK MIX

PREP TIME: 5 minutes
COOK TIME: 3½ hours (LOW)

  3 cups corn or rice cereal squares
  2 cups oyster crackers
  1 package (5 ounces) bagel chips, broken in half
1½ cups mini pretzel twists
  1 cup pistachio nuts
  2 tablespoons grated Parmesan cheese
  ¼ cup (½ stick) butter, melted
  1 package (1 ounce) dry ranch salad dressing mix
  ½ teaspoon garlic powder

1. Combine cereal, oyster crackers, bagel chips, pretzels, nuts and Parmesan cheese in **CROCK-POT®** slow cooker; mix gently.

2. Combine butter, salad dressing mix and garlic powder in small bowl. Pour over cereal mixture; toss lightly to coat. Cover; cook on LOW 3 hours.

3. Remove cover; stir gently. Cook, uncovered, 30 minutes.

Asian Beef Stew

MAKES 6 SERVINGS | **PREP TIME:** 10 minutes
COOK TIME: 5½ hours (LOW)

    2 onions, cut into ¼-inch slices
1½ pounds beef round steak, sliced thin across the grain
    2 stalks celery, sliced
    2 carrots, peeled and sliced or 1 cup peeled baby carrots
    1 cup sliced mushrooms
    1 cup orange juice
    1 cup beef broth
    ⅓ cup hoisin sauce
    ½ tablespoon cornstarch
    1 to 2 teaspoons Chinese five-spice powder or curry powder
    1 cup frozen peas
      Hot cooked rice
      Chopped fresh cilantro (optional)

1. Place onions, beef, celery, carrots and mushrooms in **CROCK-POT®** slow cooker.

2. Combine orange juice, broth, hoisin sauce, cornstarch and five-spice powder in small bowl. Pour into **CROCK-POT®** slow cooker. Cover; cook on HIGH 5 hours or until beef is tender.

3. Stir in peas. Cook 20 minutes longer or until peas are tender. Serve with hot cooked rice, and garnish with cilantro.

Thai Chicken

MAKES 6 SERVINGS

PREP TIME: 10 to 15 minutes
COOK TIME: 8 to 9 hours (LOW) or
3 to 4 hours (HIGH)

2½ pounds chicken pieces
1 cup hot salsa
¼ cup peanut butter
2 tablespoons lime juice
1 tablespoon soy sauce
1 teaspoon minced fresh ginger
Hot cooked rice (optional)
½ cup peanuts, chopped
2 tablespoons chopped fresh cilantro

1. Place chicken in **CROCK-POT®** slow cooker. Mix together salsa, peanut butter, lime juice, soy sauce and ginger in small bowl; pour over chicken.

2. Cover; cook on LOW 8 to 9 hours or on HIGH 3 to 4 hours or until done.

3. Serve over rice, if desired, topped with sauce, peanuts and cilantro.

VOLUME MEASUREMENTS (dry)

$\frac{1}{8}$ teaspoon = 0.5 mL
$\frac{1}{4}$ teaspoon = 1 mL
$\frac{1}{2}$ teaspoon = 2 mL
$\frac{3}{4}$ teaspoon = 4 mL
1 teaspoon = 5 mL
1 tablespoon = 15 mL
2 tablespoons = 30 mL
$\frac{1}{4}$ cup = 60 mL
$\frac{1}{3}$ cup = 75 mL
$\frac{1}{2}$ cup = 125 mL
$\frac{2}{3}$ cup = 150 mL
$\frac{3}{4}$ cup = 175 mL
1 cup = 250 mL
2 cups = 1 pint = 500 mL
3 cups = 750 mL
4 cups = 1 quart = 1 L

VOLUME MEASUREMENTS (fluid)

1 fluid ounce (2 tablespoons) = 30 mL
4 fluid ounces ($\frac{1}{2}$ cup) = 125 mL
8 fluid ounces (1 cup) = 250 mL
12 fluid ounces ($1\frac{1}{2}$ cups) = 375 mL
16 fluid ounces (2 cups) = 500 mL

WEIGHTS (mass)

$\frac{1}{2}$ ounce = 15 g
1 ounce = 30 g
3 ounces = 90 g
4 ounces = 120 g
8 ounces = 225 g
10 ounces = 285 g
12 ounces = 360 g
16 ounces = 1 pound = 450 g

DIMENSIONS

$\frac{1}{16}$ inch = 2 mm
$\frac{1}{8}$ inch = 3 mm
$\frac{1}{4}$ inch = 6 mm
$\frac{1}{2}$ inch = 1.5 cm
$\frac{3}{4}$ inch = 2 cm
1 inch = 2.5 cm

OVEN TEMPERATURES

250°F = 120°C
275°F = 140°C
300°F = 150°C
325°F = 160°C
350°F = 180°C
375°F = 190°C
400°F = 200°C
425°F = 220°C
450°F = 230°C

BAKING PAN SIZES

Utensil	Size in Inches/Quarts	Metric Volume	Size in Centimeters
Baking or Cake Pan (square or rectangular)	8×8×2	2 L	20×20×5
	9×9×2	2.5 L	23×23×5
	12×8×2	3 L	30×20×5
	13×9×2	3.5 L	33×23×5
Loaf Pan	8×4×3	1.5 L	20×10×7
	9×5×3	2 L	23×13×7
Round Layer Cake Pan	8×1½	1.2 L	20×4
	9×1½	1.5 L	23×4
Pie Plate	8×1¼	750 mL	20×3
	9×1¼	1 L	23×3
Baking Dish or Casserole	1 quart	1 L	—
	1½ quarts	1.5 L	—
	2 quarts	2 L	—